BRIDGING THE GAP

AF719363

BRIDGING THE GAP

CREATING A NEW PARADIGM:

A Life Care Expert's Guide for Attorneys, Trustees, and Financial & Wealth Professionals

PATRICIA A. HANSON, LPC

Patricia Hanson, LPC

BRIDGING THE GAP

CREATING A NEW PARADIGM:

A Life Care Expert's Guide for Attorneys, Trustees, and Financial & Wealth Professionals

All rights reserved
Copyright © 2026 by **Patricia Hanson, LPC**

No part of this publication may be reproduced, distributed, or transmitted in any form or by any means, including photocopying, recording, or other electronic or mechanical methods, without the prior written permission of the publisher, except in the case of brief quotations embodied in critical reviews and certain other noncommercial uses permitted by copyright law.

Cover Design: Jessica Parsons
Interior Design: Karolina Kruk-Umięcka

This book is intended for informational and educational purposes only. It does not constitute legal, financial, or medical advice. Readers should consult with qualified professionals for guidance specific to their circumstances.

Published in the United States of America

Published by Spines Publishing Platform
ISBN: 979-8-90223-631-3

Spines

CONTENTS

AUTHOR'S NOTE

Nearly 70% of Americans turning 65 today will require some form of long-term care, yet only about one-third have a plan for their elder years. Every day, I see the consequences of that gap.

I am a Life Care Expert. I sit in hospital rooms, court corridors, and living rooms where the plan on paper collides with the reality of human need. This book is a record of patterns I have witnessed and insights you can trust. It explains why crisis so often takes control and what it takes to change that.

If you are an attorney, trustee, or wealth professional, you already carry the weight of outcomes you cannot always predict. I am inviting you to view those realities through my lens and, by so doing, act with greater clarity.

You will not find busy work here. Instead, you will find useful language, standards, and stories that give you a perspective you cannot unsee once it is revealed. This book is an invitation to lead differently and to protect real people: not only older adults but also individuals with disabilities, children with special needs, and the families who love them.

We can do better, not by filling out more forms or paperwork but by having courage, clarity, and a partner on the ground who knows what to do when the plan meets the person.

This book shares professional judgment and lived experience. It is educational but does not provide legal, medical, or financial advice. Readers should rely on their own counsel, standards, and clinical guidance. Laws, standards, and policies vary by state and institution. When safety is at risk, always follow firm protocol and the applicable law.

Each chapter includes:

- Real-world case studies
- Practical insights and frameworks
- Key takeaways to reinforce learning

This book is not a technical manual. It provides a strategic framework for professionals who want to move beyond fragmented service delivery toward providing coordinated, dignified support.

Use this book both as a reference and as a guide to shifting from a crisis mindset to a proactive one where dignity and a quality of life are not left to chance. With the support of a Life Care Expert who is most frequently, a licensed professional such as a registered nurse, licensed professional counselor, or social worker, you can move beyond reacting to emergencies and instead design systems that anticipate and prevent them, while building a legacy that protects your clients in comprehensive ways.

INTRODUCTION

BRIDGING THE GAP

A quiet crisis is unfolding across our culture, one that legal documents and financial statements alone cannot resolve. It reveals itself in hospital rooms, at kitchen tables, in long-term care facilities, in bathrooms, and on front porches.

It erupts in the moment when even the best-laid plans fall short—not because they were flawed but because they did not account for the full reality of human life.

As a licensed professional counselor who has supported older adults, individuals with disabilities, and children with special needs for nearly 15 years, I have witnessed this collision between planning and humanity. I have worked alongside attorneys, fiduciaries, trustees, and wealth advisors. I have sat in family meetings where trust documents became irrelevant under the weight of crisis.

I have seen the ripple effects of unmanaged mental health, chronic illness, aging, and disability - factors that can unravel even the most thorough plan when professionals operate in isolation.

And I have reached one conclusion: we need a new model, a new paradigm, a new path forward.

Not a replacement for legal or financial best practices but a framework that integrates those essential elements, breaks down silos, and incorporates care coordination and relational insights to improve quality of life over time.

This need is not just anecdotal. The data is impossible to ignore:

- Nearly 70% of Americans over 65 will need long-term care, yet only one-third have formally prepared for it.

- Elder financial exploitation costs families and systems an estimated $2.9 billion annually.

- One in five Medicare patients is readmitted to the hospital within 30 days, costing $26 billion each year; much of this hospital care is preventable with structured oversight.

Professionals want to do the right thing. But they are often constrained by the limits of their training, the boundaries of their role, or the complexity of modern family systems. We were taught to protect assets and execute documents, not to manage lives in motion.

This book is an invitation to do both.

It is grounded in the lived tension between intention and outcome. It is built from years of collaboration with professionals across law, finance, healthcare, and the courts. It offers a proven approach for professionals ready to lead differently, think systematically, and deliver more sustainable outcomes.

This is not a manual: it is a mirror. A reference tool you can return to after reading.

It challenges us to go deeper, to redefine what fiduciary support intends to accomplish, and to address what documents alone cannot provide.

This is a call to leadership.

It is an opportunity to elevate your practice, expand your impact, and contribute to a more unified, person-centered future, one where legal and financial protections are inseparable from the preservation of dignity and the quality of life.

One where professionals lead with insight and intention and where dignity is not an afterthought but is built into the process from the start.

Join me in creating this new paradigm.

Welcome to Bridging the Gap.

Let's begin.

PART ONE

BRIDGING CRITICAL GAPS IN CLIENT SUPPORT

Eventually, every plan collides with reality. The documents may be flawless, but the person they were created to support becomes more fragile than the paperwork can contain.

This is the moment when professionals discover that legal and financial structures, no matter how strong, cannot hold the weight of human complexity. Health declines. Caregivers' burnout. Families fractured. And the plan that seemed airtight on paper begins to show its cracks.

In Part One we examine the blind spots that make even the best written documents or financial plan incomplete. Here, we begin building the framework that protects not just wealth, but quality of life itself.

CHAPTER 1

THE MISSING PIECE IN CLIENT SUPPORT: WHY CRISIS IS INEVITABLE WITHOUT COMPREHENSIVE INSIGHT

This book does not suggest an expansion of legal fiduciary duty or professional scope into care giving or clinical oversight. Fiduciary, legal, and financial professionals are not responsible for managing a client's wellbeing.

Understanding how to build plans that remain stable in the face of real life, including the realities of aging, disability, and long-term care matters as our population ages. Care needs can break down and clients become vulnerable, even when legal and financial plans are technically in place. The framework outlined in this book is designed to help professionals recognize care related risk earlier, ask better questions, and connect clients to appropriate support through qualified care professionals.

THE INVISIBLE GAP IN PROFESSIONAL SERVICES

What if the greatest vulnerabilities to your clients are not hidden in the markets or buried in the fine print of legal documents but in the quiet spaces of their daily lives? What if the real test of a plan is not whether the paperwork is correct but whether the person it was built for is safe, supported, and seen? What if quality of life itself could be elevated to the level of best practice, right alongside compliance? This is not about replacing what you already do well. It is about completing it. This presents a new paradigm, one that connects financial stability and legal safeguards to everyday lived experience.

As professionals, we may notice subtle warning signs. A client becomes isolated. Spending patterns increase. A decision looks irrational or driven by fear. Without structure or support, it is hard to know what to do with those observations. Too often, the instinct is to minimize or delay confronting what is unfolding. It's tempting for professionals to look away, but ignoring warning signs only increases risk and leaves the client more vulnerable. It is important to pause and ask deeper questions.

Traditional client support has been defined by isolated excellence. Attorneys draft precise documents. Trustees steward assets. Advisors design long-term strategies. Clinicians treat specific diagnoses. Each role is essential. But none of them alone ensures day-to-day stability. Complex care requires more than a checklist. It requires a system that weaves these threads together so that the work already being done connects to the lived reality of the person at the center.

THE MULTIDIMENSIONAL NATURE OF QUALITY OF LIFE

Quality of life is not defined by financial stability alone. It includes physical health, emotional well-being, autonomy, and the ability to participate meaningfully in daily life and relationships.

Consider these scenarios:

- **The Isolated Elder:** An aging client with an excellent estate plan quietly declines. Missed appointments, confusion, and self-neglect go unnoticed. Financial security is intact, but quality of life deteriorates.
- **The Underutilized Trust:** A child with special needs has a well-funded trust, yet no one advocates for therapies, education, or life skills programming. Funds sit untouched while opportunities for growth are lost.
- **The Overwhelmed Power of Attorney:** A devoted family member accepts professional responsibility but lacks the knowledge, time, or support to manage care

demands. Stress builds. Decisions suffer. Burnout becomes inevitable.

- **The Crisis Call:** A client appears stable during annual reviews until a sudden hospitalization, mental health breakdown, or abuse allegation exposes their vulnerability. Legal and financial structures exist, but no one has monitored the warning signs.

These are not rare scenarios. They illustrate how quickly gaps appear when human reality is left unmonitored.

BEYOND FINANCIAL ALLOCATION: WHY PLANNING ALONE IS NOT ENOUGH

A dignified life requires more than allocating funds wisely. It requires intentional coordination. Financial planning is foundational, but it is only one part of the picture. Clients need support that adapts as their circumstances evolve.

Take senior living arrangements. Independent living, assisted living, or home care can be listed as options in a plan, but each carries emotional, medical, and relational consequences invisible on paper. A "reasonable" budget line can place someone in an environment that accelerates decline, isolates them from family, or erodes their sense of identity.

These are not just housing choices: they are life decisions that affect autonomy, safety, and well-being. A comprehensive approach considers medical needs, daily functioning, financial sustainability, mental health, environmental safety, and social connection.

This is the difference between a plan that protects wealth and one that protects life. The best plans protect the person behind the plan.

KEY CONSIDERATIONS FOR PROFESSIONALS

- Recognize that legal and financial documents alone cannot safeguard dignity
- Ask how care oversight is structured for each client, not just planned
- Include the human dimension in every professional responsibility discussion

Recognizing these gaps is only the beginning. The real challenge is creating systems that prevent crises before they start.

CHAPTER 2

FROM FIREFIGHTING TO PREVENTION: WHY PROACTIVE INFRASTRUCTURE MATTERS IN COMPLEX CLIENT LIVES

SYSTEMS BUILT FOR PLANNING, NOT COMPLEXITY

Most legal, financial, and professional systems are designed for structure and planning. That part we do well. But they are not built to carry the emotional and practical weight that emerges when a client's life becomes unpredictable, unstable, or deeply complex.

When life becomes complicated, responsibility often shifts quietly onto the professionals left standing. Without a clear process in place, the response is almost always the same: it is reactive, inconsistent, and exhausting.

Repeated experiences with client crises make one reality clear: without proactive systems, preventable emergencies will continue to dominate professional practice. Over time, I have come to recognize that crisis is not inevitable. It only feels that way when no proactive system exists to identify and address unmet needs before they erupt into emergencies.

WHAT A PROACTIVE SYSTEM REQUIRES

What clients need is not more late-stage intervention. What they need is earlier structure, which can be provided by a system trained to notice and willing to lean in when the instinct is to look away.

Eighty percent of the calls we receive from professionals are crisis calls after multiple hospitalizations or a sharp decline in the person's well-being, and the family is stretched past its breaking point.

Professionals are often called in only after a situation has escalated into a full crisis; they are then forced to respond to issues that have been building unnoticed for far too long. Most would agree this is not the role any of us want to play. Fiduciary oversight is most effective when it is preventive, not reactive. In other words, **fiduciaries protect with prevention. Be the smoke detector, not the fire department.**

When a system is proactive, three elements are always present:

- Early detection of unmet needs or decline
- Structured monitoring of emerging problems
- Professional partnership to recognize subtle changes before they escalate

Without a framework built around these three elements, even diligent professionals are forced into reaction after stability has already been lost.

Professionals who engage Life Care Experts early shift into a different role. Together we become like smoke detectors, steady and ready in the background, addressing needs early, and triggering a calm, coordinated response.

WHY THIS MATTERS

Having served families both in crisis and not in crisis, I know the difference. When unmet needs smolder unseen, they erupt into crises that drain resources, fracture families, and strip away dignity. By the time we rush in with sirens blaring, many choices are no longer options, there are too many concerns to address in a short amount of time, and dignity is often at risk.

Proactive oversight changes the outcome entirely. It preserves stability before it unravels. It protects quality of life before it becomes fragile. It saves money but, more importantly, fosters trust between professionals, families, and the people at the center of the plan.

This is not about adding more work. It is about shifting when and how we engage. The opportunity is simple but profound: notice earlier, act sooner, and protect everyone involved.

PAPER PLANS VS. LIVED REALITY

Legal documents and financial plans are essential. They preserve assets, define authority, and withstand legal challenge. But they are not sufficient.

They do not see when someone is skipping their medication. They do not notice when a caregiver is running on fumes. They do not identify when a home environment has become unsafe.

These are the quiet moments where stability begins to unravel. They are not dramatic. They are easy to miss. Left unrecognized, they become the starting point for preventable crises that cost far more in dollars, in time, and in dignity than early intervention ever would.

A system of proactive oversight connects what exists on paper to what unfolds in daily life. It ensures that the work of attorneys, trustees, and advisors is not left exposed to the unpredictability of human reality.

TWO EXAMPLES THAT REVEAL THE GAP

SPECIAL NEEDS TRUSTS

When a special needs trust is created, it is always tied to a story: a diagnosis, a set of challenges, and a family's hope for stability. Yet those details are not always clear in the information that professionals receive.

The documents outline authority. Investment strategy protects the corpus. But the daily realities that shape quality of life are often unknown, usually undefined, and almost never measured.

In my work, a common scenario begins with a call from a trustee asking for support with a beneficiary. My first questions are always about the basics: the person's age, where they live, who supports them, how they function day to day, the public programs they rely on, and the diagnosis that led to the creation of the trust.

Most often, the trustee cannot answer these questions. The diagnosis is unclear. The understanding of the beneficiary's daily life is vague. Functional ability is undefined until we step in, gather the information, document it, and create a dynamic plan.

When professionals make decisions based on partial or unreliable information, the results are predictable: preventable crises, accelerated decline, and dignity lost in ways no trust was ever meant to allow.

FAMILY CAREGIVER COLLAPSE

Another common breakdown occurs when a caregiver is quietly stretched beyond capacity. On paper, the bills are paid, finances are stable, and medical providers are engaged. But each and every day, the spouse or adult child is carrying the full weight of daily care.

These family members are losing sleep, missing their own appointments, and suffering from isolation and depression. Jobs are disrupted. Health is compromised. Yet because nothing "official" appears wrong; no intervention occurs.

Then one day, the caregiver cannot continue. Sometimes they themselves are hospitalized. Sometimes it is burnout that leads to a sudden refusal to go on. Either way, the system collapses overnight, and professionals are left scrambling to rebuild stability from the ground up.

Both scenarios reveal preventable breakdowns. They show how costly it is to overlook early signs of unmet needs and caregiver strain.

KEY CONSIDERATIONS FOR PROFESSIONALS

As we review the gap, here are questions to ask yourself:

- Am I serving primarily as a crisis responder or as a long-term strategy partner?
- Have I built systems that allow me to act early, or do I only react once stability has been lost?
- Who on my team can detect the early signs of decline before they become emergencies?

Even with these questions in mind, one issue remains: Who is best positioned to carry out this kind of proactive oversight?

The answer is a Life Care Expert, whose professional role bridges the gap that existing systems cannot. The Life Care Expert's mandate is to stand in the gap, integrating care, while supporting legal, and finance offering insight that creates one coordinated system.

Professionals protect best through prevention.

Attorneys, trustees, and wealth managers already carry the responsibility for achieving outcomes that remain invisible until it is too late. Without a proactive infrastructure, professionals are trapped in a reactive cycle that drains finances, destabilizes families, and erodes client dignity. And with clients aging and leaving behind adult children with disabilities or grandchildren with special needs, the complexity will only increase.

The absence of infrastructure does not just create frustration: it creates exposure. The missing system leaves fiduciaries, attorneys, and financial professionals without the tools they need to protect dignity. The next chapter introduces the Life Care Expert; the role built to carry this responsibility and bridge the gaps that systems alone cannot close.

CHAPTER 3

THE LIFE CARE EXPERT: BRIDGING CRITICAL GAPS IN CLIENT SUPPORT

PREVENTION AS A SYSTEM

As we explored in the previous chapter, the lack of infrastructure forces professionals into a reactive stance. Fiduciary, legal, and financial systems were never designed to carry this kind of weight. When they operate without coordinated oversight, both families and professionals can become overwhelmed.

Most professional systems are well suited for predictable needs. They are not designed for the speed and complexity of decline, especially when a client's life becomes unstable, unpredictable, or deeply complex. When things begin to unravel and no one is positioned to act, the response is reactive.

Prevention is not an abstract concept. It rests on four core practices:

- Structured assessment
- Implementing plans to address unmet needs
- Ongoing monitoring
- Proactive maintenance

Assessment identifies risks early. Implementation resolves gaps. Monitoring tracks changes before they become emergencies. Proactive maintenance ensures that medical, legal, financial, and daily life decisions remain aligned. Together, these practices transform prevention from an idea into a comprehensive system.

When no proactive system exists, the results are predictable:

- Trust officers become emotional first responders.
- Attorneys are pulled into family dysfunction beyond their role.
- Fiduciary resources are consumed by one avoidable crisis after another.
- Vulnerable individuals end up over-medicated, under-resourced, or entirely unsupported in a system that protects itself more than it protects them.

We are not failing; though the stress can feel like we are, we are operating inside systems that were never designed to carry this kind of weight. The solution is a role built for integration.

WHY "LOOKING AWAY" SIGNALS A SYSTEMIC GAP

When the realities of decline due to aging, a disability-related concern, mental health concerns, or family breakdown surface, professionals may first want to minimize the problems or delay confronting the unfolding crisis. As professionals we don't have the luxury of looking away. Ignoring the signs only increases risk and leaves the client more vulnerable. You may notice a client becoming more isolated, a caregiver showing exhaustion, or a report that does not make sense. In the moment, it may feel easier to move on to the next demand of your day. The urge to look away signals the absence of a structure to act on early warning signs. Without that framework, small issues build quietly until they erupt into crisis.

What is missing is not more documentation or more rules but a professional role that bridges care and medical realities, financial stability, legal safeguards, and the lived experience of vulnerable clients.

BRIDGING THE GAP BETWEEN PLAN AND REALITY

The work of Life Care Experts is not an "add-on" service. We address unmet needs that appear when a plan requires more than paperwork to be effective. Our work is most powerful when we sit at the same table with legal, financial, and fiduciary professionals from the start, not as an afterthought. Our presence bridges the gap between planning and daily life.

Life Care Expert's are professionals who integrate care management, medical advocacy, and interdisciplinary coordination into fiduciary, legal, and financial ecosystems. They may be aging life care professionals, medical advocates, and others with training and experience to manage complex care needs. While focusing on prevention, stability, and quality of life, Life Care Experts provide the insight that fiduciaries and families need to protect both people and plans. In this book, the terms "Life Care Expert" and "care manager" are sometimes used interchangeably.

Many assume that the role of a Life Care Expert is to provide case management, just under a different name. It is not. Case management was never designed to integrate fiduciary, legal, and financial oversight into one system of care. Traditional case management provides important support but does not carry fiduciary accountability or integrates care with legal and financial realities.

Although the role of Life Care Expert is rooted in the field of care management, they are professional who go beyond to integrate care, medical, psychosocial, fiduciary, and legal realities and ensure that they are aligned.

PROFESSIONAL FOUNDATIONS OF LIFE CARE EXPERTS

The Life Care industry began in the late 1970s and 1980s, when nurses, social workers, and other professionals helped families coordinate services and navigate aging and disability. Over time, professional training, a code of ethics, and standards developed.

Life Care Experts are not defined by a single license or state credential. They often hold advanced degrees and professional licenses such as RN, LPC, LCSW, or LSW. These educational backgrounds ensure that those serving in this role bring both formal training and practical experience. Many are members of the Aging Life Care Association (ACLA) or medical advocacy associations.

Our life care management firm goes one step further by hiring trained fiduciaries. They provide some fiduciary services (POA and routine bill payment) to our clients, train our clinical team to understand the fiduciary role, and understand the care needs of our clients as well. We use care management industry-standard software systems and comprehensively document client needs, services, and outcomes. This dual foundation of fiduciary training and structured documentation creates oversight that protects both client well-being and fiduciary standards. We also carry professional fiduciary insurance.

For professionals, this provides assurance that a Life Care Expert is not simply a care manager but a professional partner who understands their professional responsibility and works to protect both the client and the fiduciary's obligations.

Life Care Experts bring:

- Cross-disciplinary insight into medical, care, behavior, and family systems.
- Oversight that addresses emergencies before they become crises.
- Navigation of medical, mental health, and environmental risks.
- Clarity and support for professionals managing emotional and complex caseloads.
- Direct coordination with family members, providers, and decision makers.
- Understanding of public programs and senior care that clients require.
- A structured, trauma informed process that prioritizes dignity and quality of life.

Sometimes people come to us early and we guide them through the process of planning for care, but most come to us in crisis, and we stabilize the situation over time. Others stabilize only long enough to manage the next wave of instability. In all cases, outcomes improve because the framework we create is designed to address unmet needs before they escalate into crisis.

THE INVISIBLE CHALLENGES

Sarah, a wealth manager with 20 years of experience, prides herself on comprehensive financial planning. Her clients' portfolios were strong, and their legal documents impeccable. Yet she soon realized that financial planning alone could not ensure the well-being of her aging clients.

One client Warren began showing signs of cognitive decline. His estate plan and investments were secure, but his daily life was unraveling. Bills went unpaid. Personal hygiene declined. His isolation deepened. Sarah recognized that even though she could manage his finances, she could not manage his care. She partnered with a Life Care Expert to create a person-centered plan. Sarah focused on financial protection, while the Life Care Expert translated those resources into practical support. Together, they ensured that Warren's resources supported both his safety and his quality of life.

A Life Care Expert draws on skills in assessment, medical and psychosocial, relationship management, and cross-system coordination. We ensure that legal, financial, and care-related plans are not just written but also lived in ways that support the person at the center.

CASE STUDY: JOHN

John was an 82-year-old living in his family home. He never married and had significant trust assets. He also had 24-hour support from a live-in caregiver Rachel, who had been with the family for years. Because of her many years of service, of loyalty, she was suggested as and eventually became his Medical Power of Attorney (MPOA). On paper, it seemed ideal: John's money was protected in trust, and his care and medical decisions were entrusted to someone who had been by his side for decades.

When the trustee requested an independent assessment from a Life Care Expert, the situation looked very different.

During the home visit, we reviewed medical, psychosocial, environmental, and financial areas of life. We noted that John was taking medications commonly prescribed for kidney disease. Yet when asked, Rachel reported that John had no medical diagnoses or conditions. This inconsistency raised immediate concern. With John's permission and a HIPAA release, we obtained his medical records. They revealed that just five months earlier, John had been hospitalized in the ICU for kidney disease and became close to requiring dialysis.

The attorneys who drafted the documents and the trustees who relied on them had unintentionally elevated Rachel into a role she was not equipped to carry. Loyalty had been mistaken for competence. Rachel lacked medical knowledge to identify and respond to significant health conditions. As a result, John remained vulnerable despite strong legal and financial protections.

For professionals, this case highlights the vulnerability created by relying on incomplete or inaccurate information provided by well-meaning caregivers. Without structured oversight, serious conditions go unrecognized until they escalate into crisis. Professionals cannot fulfill their duty to act in a client's best interest without accurate health information and professional insight to interpret it.

Too often, professionals are left to rely on secondhand reports or what is written in documents, without being able to observe or otherwise learn about the client's daily life and living conditions. The Life Care Expert bridges that gap. We bring forward accurate facts and observations, ensuring that decisions are grounded not only in paperwork but also in lived reality.

The impact can be profound. A decision based on only a partial understanding of the situation can trigger decline, while structured oversight ensures that decisions are informed, accurate, and protective.

The next chapter explores why traditional case management, though valuable, is not usually enough to meet fiduciary needs. Case managers provide important support in specific contexts, but they lack the sustained presence required to carry professional responsibility over time. Understanding the nuanced difference is essential for professionals who want to move beyond fragmented support to build a true system of protection.

CHAPTER 4

WHY TRADITIONAL CASE MANAGEMENT IS NOT ENOUGH: PARTNERING FOR QUALITY OF LIFE AND DIGNITY

THE ALLURE OF NATIONAL FIRMS

The systemic gaps described in Chapter 2 and the challenges explored in Chapter 3 might seem like problems that case management could solve. Yet case management, while valuable, was never created to serve as the structural solution. In this chapter, we explore why its role, as important as it is, cannot bridge the larger gap.

"We work with a national firm." I often hear this from fiduciaries, trust officers, wealth managers, and estate attorneys. It is said with confidence, as if this choice itself has solved the problem.

But here is the truth no one wants to say: in my experience, most national case management firms are not built to solve the real problems that professionals face.

At first glance, national case management firms appear to be the perfect solution. They offer staff who may be leaders in their field, consultants in multiple states, a centralized intake process, and a large footprint. To a busy fiduciary or institutional advisor, that all looks like relief. National vendors may offer a sense of safety to professionals working within large financial institutions. Yet when cases become increasingly complex, even the strongest systems benefit from local insight and relational depth.

CASE MANAGEMENT VS. CARE MANAGEMENT

Case management is a standard model of support, but it is often mistaken for care management. In practice, they operate on different levels.

Case management typically involves administrative coordination. It includes assessments, referrals, monitoring, and documentation, but much of this work is performed at a distance. Oversight may occur through structured check-ins, standardized protocols, and remote updates. This approach can work when client needs remain predictable, are low risk, and are self-reported accurately.

But human needs are rarely static. When circumstances shift, case managers often lack the flexibility and local connection to respond effectively. Warning signs can be missed until a crisis erupts.

Care management, in contrast, is dynamic and relationship centered. A Life Care Expert typically maintains a smaller caseload, often 15 to 25 clients, compared to the 80 to 100 or more assigned to many case managers. This lower ratio allows for deeper engagement.

Life Care Experts do not simply check in from afar. We meet directly with clients and their support systems, where they live. We observe how plans function in real life and adjust proactively. We build trust and coordinate across medical, legal, and financial domains, rather than waiting for red flags. Our value lies not only in process but also in presence. We also ensure that clients maximize public benefits and services available in their communities.

TWO CASE STUDIES

MARTHA'S STORY: OVERSIGHT AT A DISTANCE

Martha began working with a large fiduciary firm when she was 55. At the time, her needs seemed straightforward. A case manager was assigned and monitored her at a distance. For a while, the system seemed to work. Monthly check-ins were documented, and these updates reassured professionals that she was stable.

As her health declined, however, the system failed to keep pace. She missed meals, skipped appointments, and withdrew socially. None of this showed up in the case manager's reports, which were limited to standardized checklists.

When a Life Care Expert became involved, there was an immediate difference. Meeting Martha in person, understanding her evolving needs, and collaborating directly with her fiduciary team stabilized her trajectory. The shift from transactional oversight to engaged partnership was the difference between ongoing crisis and sustainable support.

MR. J.'S STORY: WHEN CASE MANAGEMENT FALLS SHORT

Mr. J. was a 72-year-old trust beneficiary with mild cognitive decline. A national case management firm was engaged, and on paper the arrangement looked sound. Monthly psychosocial check-ins were completed, and reports suggested stability.

But the case manager failed to notice that Mr. J. was skipping medications, isolating himself, missing medical appointments, and failing to pay his bills. His apartment contained unopened pill bottles and late rent notices. Within three months, he was hospitalized for dehydration and disorientation, and eviction proceedings had begun. The trustee first learned of these problems through panicked family calls, not the case manager's reports.

The family believed the trust had professionals in place, yet the system broke down. The trustee's credibility suffered, and preventable crises became unavoidable. This is the risk of case management at a distance.

THE INVISIBLE DIMENSION OF CLIENT WELL-BEING

In my work, I see a persistent disconnect between estate and financial planning and true human well-being. Attorneys and wealth managers often define success by portfolio growth, tax efficiency, and estate preservation. These are critically important, but they do not guarantee quality of life.

A client's life can unravel even when the paperwork looks perfect. Without a system that connects legal and financial safeguards to daily realities, warning signs remain unseen.

This raises an important question: How do we define compliance? Should professional responsibility be defined only by legal and financial defensibility, or should it also extend to ensuring the client is safe and supported, and that quality of life is actively monitored?

When quality of life becomes part of compliance, professionals move beyond managing portfolios and documents to protecting people.

ANOTHER CASE STUDY: ELEANOR'S STORY, A LIFE ON PAPER VS. A LIFE IN REALITY

Eleanor was an 84-year-old widow. On paper, she was secure. Her estate plan was meticulous, her investments strong, her trustee reputable.

In reality, she was isolated and declining. Her only child had died ten years earlier. Mobility challenges confined her to her home. Bills went unpaid. A leaking refrigerator left water on the floor. She was eating crackers in the dark after her electricity was shut off.

When a Life Care Expert intervened, the full picture emerged. Her home was unsafe. She was malnourished, unbathed, and grieving. With intervention, she spent two months in a respite apartment, her home was repaired, aides supported her daily life, and counseling reconnected her emotionally. Soon she was cooking again, laughing, and sharing stories about her family.

Her trustee had fulfilled every legal and financial obligation, but without care oversight, Eleanor's life was characterized by survival, not dignity.

WORKING WITH A LIFE CARE EXPERT

It is not always easy to find out how Life Care Experts truly work with clients. Brochures and websites rarely reveal the depth of practice. The difference shows up in posture, presence, and practice. Do they lean in with curiosity? Do they connect immediately with the well-being of the person at the center? Or are they focused only on intake forms and note taking?

When evaluating whether a professional is truly operating at the level of a Life Care Expert, professionals can ask these questions:

- How do you begin a relationship with a new client, and what do you look for first?
- Can you share a time you noticed something small that shifted the plan, and how you responded?
- How quickly after a referral do you meet a client in person, and how often in the first 90 days?
- Which domains do you assess, and how do you translate findings into written plans?
- What early indicators do you track that most professionals miss?
- How do you communicate with trustees and align recommendations with trust purpose?
- What is your average caseload, and how do you ensure coverage when a professional is unavailable?

- Which local resources have you engaged recently, and how do you vet them?
- What outcomes do you track beyond crisis avoidance, and how do you report them?
- How do you escalate care when a fall, medication error, or caregiver collapse occurs?
- How do you handle consent, HIPAA releases, and privacy with professionals?
- What technology supports your documentation, and how can professionals access updates?
- What feedback do you receive most often about cost and value?

A simple fit test can be revealing. Present a brief scenario to the Life Care Expert and ask for a concise two-minute response:

"A 78-year-old with diabetes has missed two medical appointments, lost five pounds in a month, and the caregiver reports poor sleep. The trustee is concerned about cost."

- A Life Care Expert would respond with immediate safety checks, a medication review, nutrition support, functional assessment, and a cost recommendation with an expected impact.

- A case manager might reschedule the medical appointments and provide educational materials.

The difference is not subtle: it is the difference between prevention and paperwork.

The stories of Martha, Mr. J., and Eleanor reveal the same truth: traditional case management records activity, but it does not prevent decline. Without proactive, relationship-based insight, blindspots erode stability and credibility.

Professional practice has long been defined by asset protection and compliance. The new paradigm demands more. It requires that quality of life be measured with the same seriousness as financial outcomes. Compliance sets the floor, but dignity must be the standard.

- This does not mean doubling workloads or stepping outside professional scope. It means engaging Life Care Experts early— professionals who connect legal, financial, and care systems so protections on paper translate into lived stability.

- Fiduciary duty has always been defined by prudence and best interest. Stopping at compliance leaves that duty incomplete. Protecting someone's future must mean more than managing their file or returning phone calls in a timely manner. It should include knowing that the person at the center is safe, supported, and seen.

Having built the case for the framework, we now turn to where it matters most: the lived experience of aging. The elder years are times of transition from working to retirement and may involve different housing situations and a move to long-term care. These are life-shaping decisions with financial, legal, and emotional consequences.

In Part Two, we examine how Life Care expertise can transform these transitions from reactive struggles into purposeful, dignified paths forward.

PART TWO

SUPPORTING OLDER ADULTS

Aging brings not only financial and medical challenges but also questions of identity, purpose, and safety. This part explores the choices and vulnerabilities that shape older adults' lives, offering strategies for stability and dignity. By integrating care, legal, and financial insight, professionals can prevent decline from becoming crisis.

Throughout this part case studies are presented as composite examples, anonymized to protect the privacy of individuals and families.

CHAPTER 5

RETIREMENT AS A MEANINGFUL JOURNEY

Modern retirement planning is no longer defined solely by the size of one's assets and it is not just about what someone can afford. It is about ensuring the richness, stability, and dignity of life in the years ahead. It is about how intentionally clients choose to live, including how they plan for finances, care, relationships, and the values that define a meaningful life.

A fulfilling and dignified retirement is anchored in several guiding principles:

- Maintaining independence while establishing a reliable safety net
- Preserving agency in financial and healthcare decisions
- Creating purposeful opportunities for growth, creativity, and service

- Strengthening personal, professional, and social support systems

Importantly, these decisions are most effective when made while individuals still have full cognitive clarity. Planning early allows couples and individuals to make value-based financial decisions with mutual understanding, instead of relying on emotional reactions later or placing the burden on others during a crisis.

A COMPREHENSIVE PLANNING FRAMEWORK

Imagine if aging and long-term care planning were approached with the same intentionality as financial or estate planning. Rather than reacting in crisis, families would engage in structured conversations about aging, care, and purpose. These conversations would directly connect to financial strategies and legal safeguards, creating a plan that integrates quality of life with sustainability.

Such a framework helps clients think not only about where they want to live and how they will pay for care but also about how dignity and purpose remain central as circumstances change. Legal and financial professionals can then translate these insights into actionable plans that align resources, expectations, and protections.

The result is a planning process that is comprehensive, proactive, and person-centered. It does more than secure finances. It secures stability, clarity, and continuity for the years ahead. Its goals are as follows:

- Reveal hidden and unconscious assumptions about aging and future needs.
- Build bridges of communication between loved ones and professional advisors.
- Make informed decisions grounded in values, rather than emotion.
- Create plans that prioritize dignity, autonomy, and sustainable well-being.
- Support solo individuals with strategies that reduce worry and improve quality of life.
- Help couples identify and reconcile different visions of retirement.
- Ensure that care decisions are made in early retirement based on financial reality, not in panic after a crisis.

KEY PILLARS OF EFFECTIVE PRE-PLANNING

HOUSING AND ACCESSIBILITY

- Evaluate home environments for safety and long-term comfort
- Explore options such as aging in place, independent living, or continuum-of-care communities

- Consider transportation needs to preserve mobility and social engagement

HEALTH AND WELLNESS OPTIMIZATION

- Integrate preventive medical planning and lifestyle strategies for vitality
- Manage chronic conditions and medication routines with intention
- Make choices that enhance long-term physical and cognitive health

DAILY LIVING SUPPORT

- Anticipate needs and costs for everyday tasks and activities
- Talk through values and preferences before a crisis emerges
- Use adaptive tools and services to preserve independence

FINANCIAL AND LEGAL READINESS

- Forecast financial needs across a lifetime, including long-term care expenses
- Align assets with personal goals and family values, rather than on emotional decisions that undermine independence
- Prepare legal documents such as powers of attorney, advance directives, wills, and trusts while capacity is fully intact

LIFE CARE EXPERTS: A STRATEGIC ALLY

Life Care Experts add a unique and essential dimension to the retirement planning process made up of the following elements:

- Deep insight into emerging care needs, costs, and practical realities
- Support for life transitions related to housing, health, or caregiving
- Advocacy for autonomy and long-term dignity
- Proactive problem solving that prevents minor issues from becoming crises
- Accurate cost modeling across categories of care, helping clients make financial choices based on foresight rather than crisis-driven emotion

JOE AND MELINDA'S STORY: FINDING CLARITY EARLY

Joe and Melinda, both in their late sixties, had just returned from a dream cruise to celebrate their anniversary. Despite their joy, they realized they were not aligned in their expectations for retirement. Joe envisioned leisure, travel, and slow mornings. Melinda, a retired social worker, wanted to stay active through teaching and volunteer work.

Their financial advisor recognized their differing visions of the future and invited them to a group session facilitated with a workbook and supported by a Life Care Expert. For the first time, they discovered how differently they viewed aging. What had once been unspoken assumptions became clear.

Fortunately, they addressed these differences while they still had full decision-making ability. Together with their advisor and Life Care Expert, they created plans grounded in clarity rather than crisis.

During the education session rather than beginning with logistics, the Life Care Expert asked the group thoughtful questions:

- What do you fear most about aging?
- What gives you a sense of meaning today, and how can that evolve?
- Whom do you feel comfortable receiving help from, and when would you ask for it?

Joe recognized that he felt unprepared to support Melinda if she became seriously ill. Melinda expressed concern that Joe might isolate or avoid seeking support. They also realized they wanted their children involved in their lives but not to the point of being overburdened with care responsibilities.

They were relieved to have this conversation while they were both cognitively strong and emotionally grounded. Their planning ensured professional clarity and reduced long-term risk, giving advisors and care experts a roadmap to protect and carve out resources while honoring the couple's quality of life.

With these insights, their planning team helped translate their vision into action:

- A senior care housing consultant identified senior living options that balanced independence with access to care.
- Their wealth advisor adjusted their retirement strategy to support both travel and healthcare.
- Their estate attorney incorporated a special needs trust for their grandson into their legacy plan.
- They named each other as Powers of Attorney, with a professional fiduciary as secondary.
- The Life Care Expert guided conversations with them and their adult children about caregiving preferences, medical choices, and long-term wishes.

PURPOSE AND PEACE OF MIND

Joe began volunteering with a veterans' organization. Melinda returned to teaching part-time. Together, they began documenting family stories for their grandson. Most importantly, they made these choices while they still had the clarity to decide with confidence. Their children were not left guessing. Instead, they were included, informed, and grateful for the intentional preparation.

LESSONS FOR PROACTIVE RETIREMENT PLANNING

ADOPT A COMPREHENSIVE PERSPECTIVE

- Financial planning should reflect emotional, physical, and social needs.
- Prepare for likely transitions, not just catastrophic possibilities.

EMBRACE MULTIDISCIPLINARY COLLABORATION

- Involve legal, financial, and care professionals in a single unified plan.
- Align stakeholders through shared language and purpose.

RECOGNIZE RETIREMENT AS A LIVING JOURNEY

- Understand that goals and needs evolve.
- Revisit plans regularly to reflect changes in health, relationships, or priorities.

BUILDING A FUTURE OF DIGNITY

Retirement is not a withdrawal from life. It is a transition that presents an opportunity to live with greater freedom, meaning, and connection. With intentional pre-planning done while cognitive abilities are intact, individuals and couples can:

- Feel secure in their decisions and supported in their independence.
- Make choices based on shared goals and values, not panic in crisis.
- Stay engaged with people, passions, and experiences that make life meaningful.

Planning for retirement is not just about money. It is a declaration of values, a commitment to quality of life, and a blueprint for how they want to be remembered. Joe and Melinda's story is a reminder that the best time to plan is when both minds are clear, voices are strong, and choices are abundant.

KEY CONSIDERATIONS FOR PROFESSIONALS

As a fiduciary, your role extends beyond financial stability. Revisit trust documents to ensure they explicitly address quality of life and best interests. Translate broad mandates into concrete oversight measures that protect dignity. Align expenditures with sustainable well-being. rather than reactive choices in crisis. Above all, encourage your clients to engage in these conversations early, while they have full clarity to shape their future with confidence. For professionals, supporting dignity at home means planning early and reducing the risks that come from waiting too long.

In the next chapter, we look at aging at home not as a choice based on emotion but as a financial decision rooted in dignity, strategy, and foresight.

CHAPTER 6

AGING AT HOME: A FINANCIAL DECISION ROOTED IN DIGNITY, NOT EMOTION

There are moments in every season of life when we must choose between holding on and moving forward. For many older adults, one of these moments is tied to the family home. A house filled with decades of memories can feel like an anchor of identity and independence. Yet beneath the warmth and nostalgia lies a financial decision with profound implications for long-term security, autonomy, and legacy.

A home is never just a physical structure. It represents belonging, history, and control. For most older adults, the desire to age at home stems from these deep emotional ties. But the gap between wanting to stay and being able to stay safely is often revealed in moments of crisis such as falls, hospitalizations, or sudden decline, when decisions are made reactively instead of strategically.

WHAT AGING AT HOME REALLY REQUIRES

Aging at home is not simply about remaining in a familiar house. It requires a coordinated plan that aligns the environment, daily support, and financial resources with the individual's changing needs. Enabling someone to remain in the home often involves modifications for safety and accessibility, reliable caregiving, and financial oversight to ensure that resources are used wisely.

The costs are significant. Home-based care can range from $52,000 to $104,000 annually for part-time support, while facility care may reach $180,000 a year, depending on the level of care required. There are also hidden costs such as home maintenance, higher utilities, and the expense of retrofitting spaces for safety. The numbers I share here are not pulled from abstract surveys. They come directly from my company's daily work supporting older adults, individuals with disabilities, and children with special needs. We shop these costs constantly, negotiating services and reviewing invoices across cases. These are not projections but the ranges of costs that fiduciaries and families are paying in today's marketplace: they represent the lived financial reality of care.

In addition to finances, it is equally important to recognize when the client is no longer safe in the home. Repeated falls, medication errors, hygiene decline, or cognitive changes create risks that overwhelm both finances and family. Professionals play a critical role in helping clients align expectations with financial resources, grounding choices in dignity rather than emotion.

THE DECISION TO MOVE

The decision to downsize or relocate rarely is made in response to a single moment. More often it emerges in quiet frustrations: the burden of yard work, the absence of first-floor laundry, or rooms long unused. Still, this refrain is commonly heard: "Maybe next year." Beneath it lies a deeper fear: If I leave, who will I be?

Reframing is essential. A move does not signal loss but can represent reclamation. Downsizing or transitioning earlier, while health and resources allow, creates freedom from burdens, preserves wealth, and positions individuals for greater security. When handled proactively, it is not surrender it is strategy.

Professionals can help clients see housing decisions as part of the broader financial and care strategy, not as an isolated lifestyle choice. Asking "Where do you want to live?" must be paired with "How do you want to live?" By reframing downsizing as a strategic decision that safeguards wealth, reduces exposure, and sustains autonomy, professionals shift the narrative from loss to possibility.

A well-timed move preserves equity, reduces ongoing expenses, and can redirect resources into trusts, investments, or prepaid care. Families often describe the outcome as liberating; they feel lighter, more secure, and more optimistic about the future.

THE HIDDEN COST OF WAITING

When planning is delayed, decisions are almost always forced by crisis. A fall or hospitalization leaves families scrambling, homes are sold under pressure, and wealth is eroded in the process. Options narrow, independence shrinks, and dignity is compromised. Waiting is not neutral. It carries real financial and emotional costs.

The reasons for delay are rarely financial. They are rooted in emotion, attachment to the family home, fear of the unknown, or the belief that "I can manage a little longer." But avoidance does not protect dignity: it often undermines it.

CASE STUDY: MARCELLA, A STORY OF WAITING TOO LONG

Marcella was 80 years old, a professional violinist who had filled concert halls with music and raised a family in the home she loved. Her house was large and elegant, but years of deferred maintenance had left it in disrepair. The roof leaked, the stairs were difficult to climb, and the heating system worked inconsistently in winter.

When Marcella's health began to decline, her son urged her to move to a safer place. She refused, insisting that with paid caregivers she could remain in her home. At first it seemed workable, but the arrangement quickly became unsustainable. Caregivers came and went. The house showed signs of neglect, and Marcella's hospitalization grew more frequent. Each discharge brought her back to the same environment, the same risks, and the same insistence that she could manage.

Eventually, Marcella's deteriorating health forced the issue. After another hospitalization, she moved to assisted living, against her will. Months later, when she had regained some strength, she quietly admitted something that stayed with me: "I should have done this years ago."

Marcella's story highlights the cost of delays. Her home, once an asset, had lost significant value. Her independence, which she had fought to preserve, was undermined by repeated crises that stripped her of control. And her son, living out of town, bore the burden of navigating difficult decisions under pressure, spending countless weekends sorting through a house that had become an overwhelming burden. What could have been a thoughtful and dignified transition became an emergency response.

For professionals, Marcella's experience underscores why these conversations cannot be postponed. Housing is not just a lifestyle decision. It is a financial, legal, and care decision with consequences that ripple across generations.

DIGNITY LIES IN THE DETAILS

Aging at home is not about remaining in one's home indefinitely; it is about living in an environment that sustains safety, autonomy, and purpose. For professionals, this is not a peripheral issue but is central to financial, legal, and fiduciary planning.

Advisors, trustees, and attorneys who help families face these decisions early preserve not only assets but also dignity. They reduce liability, prevent destabilization, and create outcomes where independence is measured not by clinging to space but by sustaining choice. Professionals who integrate purpose into planning protect more than assets: they protect the quality of life itself.

Next, we turn to the next layer of planning: avoiding care-related missteps that erode both resources and quality of life. Just as housing decisions require foresight rather than reaction, care planning demands strategy over crisis response. Together, these decisions form the framework of a system where dignity is not left to chance but is supported by a professional partnership.

CHAPTER 7

NAVIGATING THE AGING JOURNEY WITH DIGNITY AND PURPOSE

Aging is not a passive process of decline but a dynamic stage of life that demands intentional navigation. Too often, individuals and families resist acknowledging the realities of growing older. They cling to independence as an identity, confuse self-sufficiency with dignity, and delay accepting help until a crisis strips them of both choice and control. This stubbornness, though understandable, often accelerates decline and makes the work of professionals more complex and difficult.

Aging is multidimensional. It involves physical shifts, emotional resilience, cognitive changes, evolving social connections, and financial responsibilities. Where traditional views focus only on loss, a more purposeful perspective sees opportunity: the chance to preserve quality of life, extend stability, and strengthen legacy. But opportunity only exists when denial does not derail planning.

THE CONSEQUENCES OF DENIAL

One of the most common mistakes individuals make is assuming that acknowledging vulnerability is a sign of weakness. In reality, the refusal to accept support often erodes dignity more than the assistance itself ever could. Older adults who refuse medication management, reject home care, or delay transitions to safer living environments often face repeated hospitalizations, financial exploitation, or deepening isolation. By the time professionals are brought in, there are fewer options, and costs are higher.

Another misstep lies in overconfidence. Many believe they can "manage just a little longer." Yet the margin for error narrows with age. A single fall can alter mobility permanently. A missed bill can unravel financial security. A prolonged period of loneliness can trigger depression or cognitive decline. Avoiding support does not preserve independence: it endangers it.

IMPORTANT MISTAKES THAT FAMILIES OFTEN MAKE

As Life Care Experts, we repeatedly see the same patterns play out across different families and circumstances:

- **Confusing help with weakness.** Accepting support does not mean the loss of independence; it is the safeguard of it. Refusing support often speeds up decline.

- **Waiting for a crisis.** Too many decisions are made after a fall, hospitalization, or emergency when choices are limited and resources are drained.

- **Maintaining a stubborn independence.** Insisting on "managing a little longer" often shifts the burden to family members or fiduciaries, creating stress and liability.

- **Avoiding conversations.** Families who refuse to talk about care needs or future plans leave professionals with little room to protect both assets and dignity.

- **Focusing only on finances.** Protecting wealth without considering health and safety undermines the very legacy families want to preserve.

By naming these mistakes openly, professionals can reframe the conversation. Proactive planning is not about taking control away. It is about ensuring that control is exercised based on resources and values while options are still available.

BECOMING MORE VULNERABLE

With age comes heightened vulnerability. Elder abuse—financial, emotional, or physical—is a persistent vulnerability.

Stubborn independence often masks the very risks it seeks to avoid. Clients who refuse oversight may unknowingly invite exploitation, neglect, or preventable harm.

Protecting older adults requires more than surface-level safeguards. It demands comprehensive frameworks: financial monitoring, structured reporting protocols, clear legal authority, and ongoing compassionate oversight from trusted professionals.

The most credible practices integrate financial and legal structures with individualized care strategies. Doing so protects not only the balance sheet but also the human being at the center. It is not enough to wait until a client or family admits they need help. By then, a crisis is often already brewing. Instead, advisors can normalize conversations about support, frame them in terms of risk management, and align them with broader goals of asset protection, stability, and legacy.

CASE STUDY: PUTTING PRINCIPLES INTO PRACTICE

Edna was 85, a retired high school English teacher who had never married and had no immediate family. She had $400,000 in an investment account and $4,000 a month in income from her pension and Social Security. Fiercely independent, she had no desire to leave her modest home.

Over time, her living environment grew increasingly unsafe. The stairs became dangerous, chores were neglected, and isolation deepened. She refused to consider assisted living, equating it with losing autonomy. After she was hospitalized, a chairlift was installed. But there remained growing concerns about whether the home could safely support her needs. Finally, she was ready to hear what her fiduciary team suggested.

They reframed assisted living as stability, not surrender. By re-creating familiar comforts in her new apartment, arranging her favorite meals, and ensuring financial security, the team built a foundation of safety and dignity.

To Edna's surprise, the move gave her new life. She discovered connection with peers, participated in group activities, and re-engaged with her community. Her financial resources stretched further than they would have if she remained at home with private care, and her risk of isolation and crisis was dramatically reduced.

Edna's story demonstrates that with thoughtful planning and compassionate communication, even the most resistant clients can embrace transitions. For professionals, the lesson is clear: framing support as a pathway to dignity rather than a threat to independence is key to effective practice.

KEY CONSIDERATIONS FOR PROFESSIONALS

For professionals guiding clients through aging, the task is not to prevent decline but to prevent denial from doing the real damage. Your role is to help families see that accepting support is not weakness but is strategy. By naming risks early, reframing transitions as stability rather than surrender, and embedding quality of life into every financial or legal plan, you preserve both assets and dignity. Aging well is not an accident. It is the outcome of courageous conversations, clear planning, and professional guidance that insists dignity remains at the center. When professionals acknowledge caregiver strain, they prevent burnout that can destabilize even the best financial and legal plans.

In the next chapter, we turn to one of the most critical crossroads in aging: the decision to change living situations. Although individuals often view this choice through the lens of emotion, professionals must recognize it as a legal, financial, and care strategy with profound implications for safety, stability, and legacy.

CHAPTER 8

NAVIGATING THE COMPLEXITIES OF LONG-TERM CARE: A JOURNEY OF DIGNITY AND FORESIGHT

Long-term care is not just a level of care to budget for, an insurance product to purchase, or a facility placement to arrange. It is a lived reality that unfolds in the daily lives of individuals, couples, and families. It develops quietly at first and then suddenly with urgency. Every family, regardless of resources or preparation, will encounter some form of long-term care need.

Former First Lady Rosalynn Carter put it plainly: "There are only four kinds of people in the world—those who have been caregivers, those who are caregivers, those who will be caregivers, and those who will need caregivers." Her words remind us that long-term care is universal. It is not a possibility to be avoided but a stage of life to prepare for.

The COVID-19 pandemic revealed how fragile our long-term care systems already were. Facilities designed to provide safety became places of isolation and, for many, profound loss. Behind every statistic was a family, a caregiver, and a professional caught between the ideals of protection and the reality of failure. For those of us working at the intersection of law, finance, and care, the lesson was unavoidable: we cannot treat long-term care planning as optional or secondary.

Preserving financial wealth without preserving dignity is an incomplete victory. The measure of the plan is not only how long the money lasts but also whether the person at the center is safe, supported, and seen.

THE EMOTIONAL AND FINANCIAL WEIGHT OF LONG-TERM CARE

The financial costs of long-term care are staggering. When an adult child steps into the caregiving role, the annual impact can exceed $100,000 once lost wages, reduced retirement savings, and out-of-pocket expenses are included. Families pay more than dollars: the hidden emotional costs are often greater. Caregiver burnout, fractured sibling relationships, and role confusion create wounds no financial statement can show.

The cost of institutional long-term care has dramatically increased in recent years. A shared room in a skilled nursing facility can exceed $14,000 each month. Assisted living often ranges from $6,000 to $11,000 a month. These expenses destabilize even well-resourced families. Trust assets intended to last decades can be depleted within years. Without careful planning, families are forced into reactive decisions that erode both resources and dignity. If they understand the realities in the early stages of retirement planning, they can make different decisions based on additional insights.

WHY EARLY PLANNING MATTERS

Decline in health or function is rarely predictable. A fall, a sudden hospitalization, or a new diagnosis can transform stability into an overnight crisis. Once that point is reached, choices narrow dramatically. Families default to whatever bed is available, rather than what best reflects the client's values and preferences.

Early planning is the only way to preserve control. It allows clients to articulate their wishes, direct how their resources will be used, and keep their family in the role of advocate rather than exhausted caregiver. Proactive planning achieves several outcomes:

- Clients retain agency over how their story unfolds, rather than being defined by circumstance.

- Crisis-driven decisions that drain finances and emotional energy are avoided.
- Families remain advocates, not overburdened caregivers forced into unsustainable roles.
- Resources are used in alignment with the client's values, and not only with clinical requirements.

Long-term care planning should not be treated as an abstract exercise in cost projection. It must be integrated into estate, trust, and financial strategies as a core component of protecting a client's life legacy.

CASE STUDY: ROBERTA'S CALL FOR HELP

Roberta is 80 years old. At age 72, she worked with her attorney to complete estate documents, giving her brother-in-law the power of attorney. He since passed away, and she is now alone with no one to act on her behalf.

Financially, she began retirement with $400,000 managed by her advisor. When her brother-in-law became ill, she used a significant portion of those funds to help him. Today, she has $230,000 left. Her home, once her safe haven, is now her greatest liability: the roof leaks, gutters are clogged, and the house has fallen into disrepair.

Roberta wants to remain at home, but she cannot afford the level of care required to stay there. Selling "as is" would mean losing critical value, but repairing the home requires funds she does not have. Meanwhile, her health continues to decline.

From her perspective, she is still "managing." From a professional lens, she is already in crisis. Her options are shrinking by the day.

Calls like Roberta's are common in our office. Families and professionals are often shocked at how quickly independence collapses into vulnerability. A home, often the largest asset, becomes both a resource and an obstacle when maintenance and planning are deferred.

If her financial advisor, an elder law attorney, and a Life Care Expert had worked collaboratively years earlier, Roberta's trajectory could have been very different. Together, they could have preserved her resources, maintained her home properly, and prepared for a thoughtful transition to supported living. Instead, she now faces reactive choices with limited options.

KEY CONSIDERATIONS FOR PROFESSIONALS

For professionals, the role is clear. You have significant influence over how clients and families experience long-term care. Financial and legal strategies shape not only the choices but also the burdens families carry. To meet this responsibility, you must do the following:

- Anticipate the point where family caregivers can no longer provide sustainable support.
- Establish structured handoff plans so care continues seamlessly as needs increase.
- Involve families as partners in oversight while ensuring they are not left to manage alone.

When you lead with foresight, you do more than protect assets. You stabilize family systems, preserve dignity, and extend the trust's ability to meet needs without depletion.

CLOSING THE GAP

Roberta's situation shows how quickly independence can collapse without foresight, leaving clients, families, and professionals cornered by crisis. Even when resources exist, they must be recognized, coordinated, and applied at the right time.

What if long-term care were not something to resist but a collaborative effort uniting legal, financial, and care expertise? With shared responsibility, it can be. No single professional can carry this burden alone. But together, we can build frameworks that protect dignity, preserve stability, and ensure continuity. Professionals who use foresight do not just react to decline but also create stability that safeguards both the person and the plan.

The next chapter turns to the financial tools that can either strengthen or undermine these efforts. We will look closely at how long-term care is paid for, the misconceptions that derail planning, and the strategic use of long-term care insurance. For attorneys, trustees, and financial advisors, understanding these funding mechanisms is essential to aligning financial security with quality of life.

CHAPTER 9

PAYING FOR CARE AND THE STRATEGIC USE OF LONG-TERM CARE INSURANCE

Professionals who support aging adults and individuals with disabilities must help clients shift their perspective on how care will be funded. Planning should not begin with product selection or asset preservation. Instead, it should start with a clear understanding of the care currently needed and the care likely to be needed in the future. The funding strategy must align with these realities, not the other way around.

Long-term care is not a hypothetical risk. For those who live into their eighties or beyond, it is a near-certainty. Support often begins gradually, with a few hours of help at home, meal preparation, or medication reminders. Over time it progresses to more intensive oversight or facility-based care. Without intentional planning, costs escalate quickly. Families are left scrambling, uncertain which assets to use and frustrated that supposed safety nets do not provide the coverage they assumed.

Professionals are in a position to prevent this scramble. By framing care planning as a collaborative process that combines financial tools, legal protections, and clinical oversight, they can help clients prepare in a way that preserves dignity, autonomy, and choice.

A CARE-FIRST STRATEGY

Care-first planning begins with the individual's functional and quality-of-life goals, not their balance sheet. What supports are needed to sustain safety, independence, and family stability? What care settings are preferred? What risks are most likely to emerge?

Only once these questions are addressed can professionals responsibly determine how to pay for that care. This approach prevents overspending on services that do not match the client's needs. It also avoids underfunding essential support. And it reduces the friction families face when decisions are made under stress. Most importantly, it ensures that financial, legal, and clinical professionals are aligned from the beginning, activating the right resources at the right time.

THE MEDICARE MISCONCEPTION

One of the most damaging myths in long-term care planning is the belief that Medicare will pay for ongoing support. Yet Medicare only covers short-term rehabilitation after hospitalization and narrowly defined home health services. It does not cover assisted living, personal care at home, or supervision for dementia-related decline.

Professionals see the consequences of this misconception all the time. Families delay planning, thinking Medicare will cover their care when the time comes. Only later do they discover that the most essential services—bathing, dressing, toileting, medication management, and safety oversight—are excluded. At that point, costs shift abruptly to private assets, family caregivers, or professionals caught unprepared.

Correcting this misunderstanding early is critical. Professionals must be direct: they must emphasize to clients that Medicare is not a long-term care plan.

UNDERSTANDING THE ROLE OF LONG-TERM CARE INSURANCE

Long-term care insurance is often purchased with good intentions but is poorly integrated into actual care planning. Clients may begin paying premiums in their fifties or sixties, only to set the policy aside without ever revisiting its terms. When care needs arise, families may hesitate to file a claim, unsure whether eligibility is met or afraid of using up the benefit too early.

As a result, many policies are underused. Benefits are lost due to late activation, confusion about coverage, or misplaced strategies to "save" the policy for a worst-case scenario. Meanwhile, families struggle with caregiving, assets erode more quickly than necessary, and the individual's quality of life deteriorates.

The truth is simple: a policy that is never activated provides no protection. Long-term care insurance is not meant to be preserved. It is meant to be used to expand choice, increase flexibility, and ease the burden on families and fiduciaries.

STRATEGIC USE OF LONG-TERM CARE INSURANCE

Professionals should approach these policies as part of a coordinated funding strategy, not as isolated products. This means the following:

- **Reviewing the policy early.** Elimination periods, benefit triggers, daily caps, and lifetime limits must be understood long before care is needed. Surprises at the point of crisis are costly.

- **Activating benefits promptly.** Most policies require impairment in two or more activities of daily living or a cognitive diagnosis before they provide benefits. Once these criteria are met, delaying activation rarely serves the client. Early use can support independence, prevent escalation, and preserve other resources.

- **Coordinating across disciplines.** Attorneys, financial advisors, and Life Care Experts each see different aspects of the picture. Only together can they align estate structures, Medicaid planning, and real-time care needs.

- **Reducing pressure on other assets.** Insurance benefits should be used to fund daily care so that other tools, such as investments, trusts, or annuities, can be preserved or repurposed for long-term stability. When managed collaboratively, these policies become more than insurance: they become leverage that sustains both quality of life and financial resilience.

CASE STUDY: THE POLICY LEFT WAITING

Thomas, age 79, had been paying into a long-term care insurance policy for more than 25 years. The policy provided four years of coverage for home care, assisted living, or memory care. When his memory began to decline and his wife could no longer manage on her own, the family did not realize that a policy existed. His financial advisor had not reviewed it with them in years. His adult children assumed that Medicare would provide what he needed.

For two years, his wife shouldered most of the care herself. She paid privately for part-time aides, dipped into their retirement savings, and stretched beyond her own health limits. Only when a hospital social worker asked about insurance did the family discover the policy. By the time a claim was filed, Thomas required memory care because he was wandering and no longer safe at home. The benefits began, but he died six months later, having used only a fraction of the four years of coverage he had faithfully paid for.

This scenario is common in my work. Policies sit in files, forgotten or misunderstood, while families struggle unnecessarily. Had the financial advisor reviewed the policy regularly and collaborated with an elder law attorney and a Life Care Expert, Thomas's benefits could have been activated earlier. Used strategically, the coverage would have provided support at home, delayed facility placement, and eased the burden on both his wife and his children. Instead, most of the policy value was lost, and the family carried a heavier burden than necessary. What if the real value of long-term care insurance was not in the policy itself but in how it was used? A benefit left untouched out of fear or confusion offers no protection. But when attorneys, financial advisors, and Life Care Experts coordinate, the policy becomes more than a check. It becomes a safeguard that preserves dignity, choice, and family stability.

Unused benefits protect no one. Activated strategically, they create conditions for care that honors dignity.

Long-term care insurance and other funding strategies can only protect clients if they are activated and managed wisely. Yet financial planning alone does not shield vulnerable adults from another growing threat: exploitation, fraud, and coercion.

The next chapter will explore how professionals can best protect clients against abuse. We will examine the warning signs of exploitation, the systems most often manipulated, and the proactive measures that attorneys, trustees, wealth managers, and Life Care Experts can take to prevent harm before it dismantles everything a client has built.

CHAPTER 10

PROTECTING CLIENTS FROM EXPLOITATION: A CALL FOR VIGILANCE, INTEGRITY, AND COLLABORATION

There is a profound responsibility at the intersection of aging, vulnerability, and trust. Not all harm to older adults comes from strangers. Too often, it comes from those they love most. Elder exploitation is not only a financial crime. It is also a breach of dignity and a betrayal of trust.

For attorneys, trustees, and wealth managers, preventing exploitation is not a peripheral issue but is a core professional responsibility. Allowing exploitation to go undetected can devastate clients, erode family legacies, and expose professionals to liability. The question is not whether exploitation will occur in the populations you serve. The question is whether you and your team will detect and stop it before the damage is irreparable.

A CASE THAT SHOULD NOT HAVE HAPPENED: DOROTHY'S STORY

The following case illustrates how exploitation hides in plain sight and why professional collaboration is essential.

Dorothy was 78 years old. Independent her entire life, she had lived alone in the home where she was born. As her health declined, she welcomed help from her closest companion, her best friend Linda.

Linda was 58 and struggling financially. She offered to move in, which at first seemed like a blessing. Soon after, her boyfriend joined them. He was not a caregiver. He was a gambler. Together, he and Linda convinced Dorothy to use her money "to make more money."

Over time, more than $750,000 disappeared from Dorothy's accounts. Withdrawals were disguised as gifts, investments, home repairs, or loans. Dorothy approved of the transactions on paper, but actually she was confused, emotionally dependent, and manipulated by those she trusted most.

Her home deteriorated. Bills went unpaid. Food spoiled in the refrigerator. Clutter and neglect consumed the living space. Neighbors noticed she no longer came outside. When Adult Protective Services (APS) intervened after Linda missed a medical appointment for Dorothy, they found a woman exploited, neglected, and silenced.

A Life Care Expert with fiduciary capacity was engaged through APS. The team assessed the situation, built trust with Dorothy, and coordinated with her elder law attorney and the district attorney. Linda and her boyfriend were removed from the home through eviction and later faced prosecution for financial exploitation.

WHAT CHANGED THE OUTCOME

Once our team engaged, everything shifted. Dorothy was relocated with her cat to a safe, supportive assisted living community, where she could receive care and regain stability. Her remaining assets were secured and reorganized by her elder law attorney to support her long-term needs. Updated documentation protected her from further manipulation.

Dorothy's story ended with safety but only after years of erosion. The financial losses could not be undone. Her choices were narrowed. Her dignity was damaged, but through careful planning her life improved. She made friends in assisted living and developed meaningful connections.

Had her attorney and financial advisor communicated with one another or engaged a Life Care Expert earlier, the warning signs could have been addressed before three-quarters of a million dollars vanished. The siloed approach allowed exploitation to flourish. Collaboration would have changed the outcome.

WARNING SIGNS PROFESSIONALS MUST RECOGNIZE

Exploitation rarely begins with a single large withdrawal of funds. Instead, it often emerges gradually, disguised as gifts, favors, or offers of help.

Physical decline paired with financial instability is often the most visible signal that something more is happening beneath the surface. Recognizing these patterns early is how professionals bridge the gap between financial safety and personal dignity.

IF YOU SEE SOMETHING, DO SOMETHING

It is not enough to collect signatures or rely on technical approvals. Exploitation often hides behind formal consent. When circumstances shift, professionals must ask hard questions. Is the client truly capable of making these decisions? Have relationships changed in ways that increase dependence or risk? Do their choices still align with their long-term stability and dignity?

And perhaps most importantly: Does your instinct as a professional suggest a different story than the one being presented? When you are unsure, the obligation is clear. Engage colleagues, investigate further, and take protective action. Silence in the face of doubt can unintentionally enable harm.

A CIRCLE OF PROTECTION, NOT A SINGLE LINE OF DEFENSE

Exploitation thrives in isolation, whereas prevention succeeds when oversight is shared. Attorneys must keep estate and financial documents updated to reflect capacity and prevent misuse. Financial advisors must treat irregular activity with scrutiny, even if transactions seem to be authorized. Early questioning can preserve assets before they are lost.

Life Care Experts bring another dimension by assessing health and environmental realities that financial records cannot show. And when safety is at risk, reporting to Adult Protective Services is not optional. A true protective circle exists only when each discipline fulfills its role and communicates with the others.

BEYOND LEGAL AUTHORITY LIES ETHICAL RESPONSIBILITY

Legal documents alone are not sufficient protection. A signed Power of Attorney or trust agreement is not a shield against exploitation. At times, these very tools are the doorway to it. Professionals must remain engaged throughout the client's journey, making time to check in directly with the client and not only through representatives.

They must look beyond what is legally permissible and ask whether choices serve the client's best interest. High-risk clients, especially those who are isolated, cognitively impaired, or increasingly dependent, require proactive safeguards. Exploitation is easier to prevent than repair, and prevention is part of a professional's fiduciary duty.

THE DIFFERENCE COLLABORATION MAKES

Dorothy's story ended safely, but not before her dignity and security were compromised. This is what happens when caregiving and financial authority go unchecked. The line between help and harm blurs, and clients are left to suffer the consequences.

Exploitation is not an anomaly it is a predictable vulnerability in every professional practice. Professionals who assume that good intentions are enough allow harm to occur in the shadows. Those who commit to collaboration, vigilance, and intervention protect more than assets. They protect lives.

What if silence is the greatest risk of all? Protecting clients from exploitation requires more than documents and signatures. It requires presence, questioning, and coordinated oversight.

KEY CONSIDERATIONS FOR PROFESSIONALS

As a fiduciary, attorney, or wealth advisor, your vigilance is not optional. Exploitation is one of the most predictable risks in aging populations yet also one of the most preventable. This means you should do the following:

- Make it routine to question sudden changes in financial behavior or new "helpers" in a client's life.

- Do not rely solely on signed documents as proof of safety; pair them with direct engagement and observation.

- Build strong collaborative systems with Life Care Experts and other professionals to ensure someone has eyes on both the finances and the daily realities of a client's life.

- Treat prevention as part of fiduciary prudence. The cost of silence is too high for assets, for reputations, and most of all, for client dignity.

By embedding vigilance into everyday practice, you protect more than wealth. You protect the trust that clients place in you and the legacy they hope to leave behind.

The next chapter examines how caregiver arrangements, particularly family caregiving and informal caregiver roles, can become breeding grounds for undue influence. By building the right frameworks, professionals can safeguard not only the client's dignity and safety but also the integrity of the fiduciary role itself.

CHAPTER 11

THE RISKS OF INFORMAL CAREGIVING: WHEN GOOD INTENTIONS AREN'T ENOUGH

The line between care and collapse is often thin for older adults. The need for physical, emotional, or logistical support can draw family members, friends, or neighbors into caregiving roles for which they were never trained or prepared. Informal caregiving, when left unstructured, creates exposures: caregiver burnout, blurred financial boundaries, medical oversights, and family conflict. What begins as generosity and love can quickly evolve into crisis when there are no systems in place to support the caregiver or the client.

Informal caregiving arrangements, even when motivated by compassion, almost always become problematic without accountability and oversight. Good intentions cannot replace structure. Without clear expectations, training, and monitoring, caregivers—whether family, friends, or privately hired—end up carrying responsibilities that exceed their capacity. The result is predictable: missed medical needs, financial missteps, caregiver exhaustion, and growing vulnerability for the client. Families may not recognize the risks until the situation has already begun to unravel.

Professionals should recognize that relying solely on informal caregiving places clients at risk. When support must extend beyond short-term recovery, the conversation should shift toward structured, accountable solutions. Identifying qualified care agencies or creating formal employment arrangements is not just a task for the family task but is also an area where professional guidance adds stability and protection.

WHY PROFESSIONAL CAREGIVERS ADD VALUE

Although family members and friends can provide meaningful support, professional caregiving structures add measurable value. Professional caregivers are trained, insured, supervised, and accountable within systems that protect both the client and the fiduciary. By steering families toward vetted care providers and insisting on documented agreements, trustees and attorneys create a paper trail that demonstrates prudence and reduces liability if disputes arise. Professionalized caregiving protects professionals as much as it protects beneficiaries.

WHY FORMAL AGREEMENTS MATTER

Protecting everyone involved with formal caregiver agreements, whether through an agency or as a member of a household staff, should be the priority. Agreements define duties, establish wages, and prohibit unauthorized access to funds or estate influence. They also clarify expectations and reduce disputes. Without them, families miss valuable tax credits and deductions available for paid caregiving. They may also face legal consequences for violating labor laws. Caregivers engaged privately outside a payroll system forfeit access to Social Security, Medicare, and unemployment protections.

For fiduciaries, these agreements are evidence of due diligence. They ensure transparency, protect clients, and safeguard professionals from accusations of negligence if something goes wrong.

THE ROLE OF AGENCIES AND PRIVATE CAREGIVERS

Families often wrestle with whether to hire through an agency or hire privately.

- **Agencies bring built-in safeguards.** They handle payroll, background checks, training, supervision, and insurance. This gives professionals and families confidence that care is delivered within a compliant structure.

- **Private caregivers offer consistency, flexibility, and sometimes higher skill levels.** But without oversight, roles can blur, and there can be missed documentation, unpaid taxes, and financial risk.

In our practice, we have seen success with both approaches. Neither is inherently better in my humble opinion: both come with trade-offs. Agencies provide very important safeguards but can feel impersonal. Private caregivers bring consistency but require strong professional oversight. A Life Care Expert adds value by helping families weigh options, draft caregiver agreements, set up payroll and tax compliance, ensure background checks, and monitor care. In many cases we use a hybrid model, where private caregivers are formally employed through an agency. This offers the safeguards of agency oversight with the consistency of their team of caregivers that families often want. The hybrid model also creates a larger pool of backup caregivers to step in during emergencies and on vacations.

RECOGNIZING THE RED FLAGS

The collapse of informal caregiving rarely happens overnight. It shows up in patterns: mounting caregiver stress, unpaid bills, missed appointments, uncharacteristic financial activity, or a caregiver speaking for the client instead of supporting their voice. Financial warning signs include inconsistent withdrawals, missing receipts, or sudden increases in spending on everyday items. Each sign may seem minor, but together they signal that a caregiving arrangement is under strain. Early intervention at this stage can prevent full collapse.

CASE STUDY: EDWARD—CARE THAT COLLAPSED WITHOUT STRUCTURE

Edward was 79 years old, a retired professor, widowed, and childless. He lived alone in the colonial home he and his wife had restored. His finances were stable and his mind sharp. But one winter, he slipped on the ice and broke his hip. Recovery was slow, and for the first time, he needed help.

A woman from his church, Clara, began visiting. She brought groceries, picked up prescriptions, and soon offered to stay overnight. Grateful and lonely, Edward welcomed her companionship. Within months, Clara had become his primary caregiver. What began as kindness soon became overwhelming. Clara had no training, no outside support, and no clear agreement about her role.

The consequences were predictable. Edward's mail went unopened, bills piled up, and medical appointments were missed. Clara casually used his money for groceries and gas, convinced she was helping. Exhausted and defensive, she resisted outside involvement. By the time professionals intervened, Edward was malnourished, his home was in disrepair, and his accounts were in disarray. His story illustrates why good intentions, without structure and oversight, cannot sustain safe, effective care.

COMPASSION REQUIRES A FRAMEWORK

Care is an act of love, but love alone is not a protection plan. Without structure and oversight, even the best-intentioned caregiving arrangements can collapse. The difference between caregiving that sustains and caregiving that unravels is not the caregiver's heart but the presence or absence of accountability and support.

For fiduciaries, compassion must be matched with structure. Partnering with Life Care Experts and vetted care providers transforms good intentions into sustainable systems. These stabilize families, protect clients, and demonstrate fiduciary prudence. In practice, professionals can point to formal caregiving arrangements as evidence that they acted in the client's best interest, balancing compassion with accountability.

KEY CONSIDERATIONS FOR PROFESSIONALS

Informal caregiving may seem natural and convenient, but without structure it places both clients and professionals at risk. As a trustee, attorney, or financial advisor, you are not expected to manage caregiving directly, but you are expected to ensure it is documented and accountable. Encourage families to formalize arrangements through caregiver agreements. These agreements provide transparency, unlock potential tax benefits, and create legal protections that informal caregiving lacks.

Partnering with a Life Care Expert brings the day-to-day visibility needed to confirm that plans are functioning in practice, not just on paper. Structured oversight creates stability for families, reduces stress for caregivers, safeguards dignity, and protects professionals from liability.

Good intentions are not enough. Sustainable care requires structure. By helping families move from informal arrangements to accountable systems, you fulfill both your professional duty and your ethical responsibility to protect clients.

In the next chapter, we turn to hospice and palliative care. Too often misunderstood as the "end of the road," these models are in fact about living fully, with dignity, comfort, and autonomy until the very end. We will examine how professionals can integrate these services into planning in ways that protect both the individual and their family.

CHAPTER 12

THE ROLE OF HOSPICE AND PALLIATIVE CARE

Conversations about hospice and palliative care are never easy. Many people resist the topic, equating it with surrender or the end. As a Life Care Expert and counselor, I approach these discussions gently, knowing that fear and misunderstanding can block access to vital support. I often begin by saying, "There is a type of care covered by Medicare that might improve your comfort and bring peace into your daily life." Framed this way, families are more open to listening and less likely to shut down.

When my team recognizes that someone may be eligible for hospice or palliative services, we explain their benefits and limitations and then help them decide whether these services could improve dignity and reduce stress. When the family is ready, we make the referral, and the hospice or palliative provider assumes the lead role while we remain in the background to support the transition.

UNDERSTANDING HOSPICE

Hospice care is often misunderstood as giving up, but in practice it is a structured system that prioritizes comfort, dignity, and quality of life for people living with chronic or life-limiting illnesses. Hospice shifts the focus from cure to comfort. Its goal is to manage pain, coordinate services, and support emotional and spiritual needs so that each day has meaning.

Hospice is designed for those with a life expectancy of six months or less if the illness runs its normal course, but eligibility can last much longer. Many clients move on and off hospice depending on how their condition changes. Far from hastening death, my experience has been that hospice often allows people to live longer and more peacefully by reducing stress and stabilizing care.

Hospice can be provided at home, in assisted living, in nursing facilities, or in hospice centers. Medicare Part A covers the cost, including medications, medical equipment, and the support of an interdisciplinary team. Families benefit from respite care, emotional counseling, and bereavement services, while patients receive regular oversight from nurses, social workers, chaplains, and aides. For many families, hospice is the first time they feel like they are no longer carrying the weight alone.

UNDERSTANDING PALLIATIVE CARE

Palliative care differs from hospice in that it can be offered at any stage of a serious illness. It is available while curative treatments continue and focuses on managing symptoms such as pain, fatigue, nausea, anxiety, or depression. The goal is to help individuals live well in the present, regardless of whether their condition is terminal.

Palliative care can be delivered in hospitals, clinics, or homes. It is often covered under Medicare Part B or Medicare Advantage plans. Like hospice, it reduces strain on families by managing symptoms and coordinating providers. For many clients, palliative care serves as a bridge, bringing relief long before they are eligible for hospice.

THE TRUE VALUE OF HOSPICE AND PALLIATIVE CARE

The true value of hospice and palliative care lies not only in symptom management but also in the relief they bring to families. These services reduce frantic late-night hospital runs, cycles of stress, and the quiet exhaustion of caregivers trying to hold everything together on their own. Skilled teams step in to share the load, creating structure where there was once chaos.

Families often describe hospice as a gift. It allows them to spend more time being present with their loved one instead of constantly coordinating medications, equipment, or emergencies. The focus shifts from survival to connection. The gift is not only comfort for the client but also relief and reassurance for those who love them.

CASE STUDY: LOUISE CHOOSING DIGNITY AGAIN AND AGAIN

Louise was 81 when her congestive heart failure worsened. She had lived independently for decades in the home where she raised her children, but her stamina was fading. Fluid built up in her lungs, hospital visits became frequent, and she felt scared and overwhelmed. Her daughter Grace tried to keep up with the increasing demands of caregiving, but the burden grew heavier with each passing month.

Louise's financial advisor referred her to a Life Care Expert who became an essential partner in her journey. After yet another hospitalization, the Life Care Expert recommended hospice. Grace hesitated, fearing hospice meant the very end. With guidance, she learned that hospice could stabilize care, relieve stress, and bring dignity now and not just in the final days.

Louise enrolled in hospice at home. Equipment and medications were delivered. Nurses visited regularly. A chaplain prayed with her, and a social worker supported the family. A caregiver came to help with bathing. Louise's breathing improved, her anxiety eased, and Grace finally felt she had a partner in the process.

Six months later, Louise stabilized and was discharged. That cycle repeated over the next six years. Each time she declined, hospice returned. Each time she improved, services transitioned back. Through it all, the Life Care Expert coordinated each transition, smoothing the process, supporting Grace, and ensuring that Louise's care aligned with her wishes.

Louise died peacefully at home, surrounded by her family. There was no frantic ER visit, no chaos—just dignity.

THE LIFE CARE EXPERT'S ROLE

When care needs change, someone must be ready to act. A Life Care Expert helps families recognize when hospice or palliative care should be initiated or restarted, preventing emergencies that force rushed hospitalizations. They coordinate with providers, support caregivers, and make sure decisions are grounded in the client's values. They facilitate difficult conversations so that families are not left guessing or overwhelmed. Above all, they ensure that hospice and palliative care are not seen as defeat but as essential supports that protect dignity and bring peace.

LIVING BETTER, NOT LESS

Hospice and palliative care are not about hastening death. They are about living better, longer, and with greater peace. They bring structure, reduce suffering, and protect dignity at times when families often feel the most fragile.

Louise's story reminds us that while we cannot control everything that happens to our bodies, we can choose how we experience what happens. Hospice and palliative care make that choice possible by creating space for comfort, connection, and peace.

KEY CONSIDERATIONS FOR PROFESSIONALS

As a fiduciary, attorney, or advisor, you are not expected to manage hospice or palliative care. But awareness of these Medicare-covered benefits matters because they reduce family stress, lower costs, and improve quality of life for clients.

Your role is to:

- **Be aware these benefits exist.** Families often delay seeking hospice or palliative care because they misunderstand it as "the end."
- **Encourage timely support.** When you hear that clients are struggling with repeated hospitalization or worsening

symptoms, remind them that these services may provide relief.

- **Connect families with expertise.** A Life Care Expert can guide them through the decision and connect them with providers.

You do not need to master the details. Simply knowing these supports exist, and encouraging families to explore them with the right experts, ensures that clients do not miss out on services that can stabilize care, safeguard resources, and protect dignity.

In the next chapter, we will explore the cognitive and behavioral challenges of dementia and Alzheimer's disease. These conditions demand not only medical expertise but also coordinated strategies to safeguard both the individual and the plan.

CHAPTER 13

UNDERSTANDING COGNITIVE AND BEHAVIORAL CHALLENGES IN DEMENTIA AND ALZHEIMER'S DISEASE: PRESERVING IDENTITY

Dementia and Alzheimer's disease are two of the most challenging journeys in aging. These conditions affect not only memory and thinking but also behavior, relationships, and the very essence of who a person is. Families often describe the experience as losing someone while they are still physically present.

For professionals, it is critical to understand dementia and Alzheimer's as more than memory loss. These conditions reshape communication, decision making, and identity. They demand compassionate, structured, and proactive care.

SEEING WHAT OTHERS MISS

Dementia and Alzheimer's are not only about forgetting names or dates. One of the most telling early indicators is a loss of executive functioning: the ability to plan, sequence, and carry out multi-step tasks. Trained eyes see what untrained observers may overlook.

A simple request like, "Tell me how you would cook an egg," can reveal the deficit. An individual may know what an egg is and where the pan is kept. But the sequencing, getting the pan, turning on the stove, adding oil, cracking the egg, waiting for it to cook, may become disorganized or stall in the middle.

To a professional who works primarily with documents or finances nothing may look wrong. Bills might still be paid, signatures look the same, and investment accounts may appear stable. But the real risk is unfolding in the client's daily life. Executive functioning deficits are not usually captured in the creation of documents or in reviewing a financial plan. They are revealed only through observation, interaction, and careful assessment.

This is where you should rely on professionals trained to connect the dots between what looks fine on paper and what may be unraveling in practice.

PROFESSIONAL IMPLICATIONS FOR PROFESSIONALS AND ADVISORS

Dementia and Alzheimer's are not only medical and family issues. They carry profound fiduciary and legal implications when left unrecognized.

Executive functioning decline often shows up long before memory lapses are obvious. This subtle erosion places professionals in a position of significant exposure. A client may still be able to sign checks or appear articulate in short conversations. Yet behind the scenes, bills go unpaid, scams are missed, medications are mismanaged, and safety erodes.

In these moments, professionals may be left exposed if oversight does not detect functional decline.

EXAMPLES OF DECLINE INCLUDE:

- A client with early dementia authorizes a questionable financial transaction. Without documentation of oversight, the professional may be accused of failing to protect the estate.

- A client continues living alone despite unsafe conditions. If injury occurs, professionals may be questioned for not intervening.

- A caregiver with informal authority lacks competence or accountability, resulting in financial exploitation or neglect.

Life Care Experts help bridge the gap. Through structured oversight and direct observation, they detect the early executive functioning changes that financial reports or legal documents cannot reveal. This protects fiduciaries, prevents unnecessary asset depletion, and ensures that interventions occur before crises force reactive, high-cost decisions.

BEYOND MEMORY LOSS

While memory loss is the most visible symptom, dementia and Alzheimer's affect multiple areas of daily functioning. Planning, organizing, and decision making become increasingly difficult. Language abilities fade, leading to word-finding struggles and eventually challenges with expressing even simple ideas. Disorientation develops—not just with places but with time itself.

These shifts erode independence and destabilize safety long before families are prepared.

BEHAVIORAL AND PSYCHOLOGICAL EXPRESSIONS

Cognitive changes are often accompanied by behavioral and psychological shifts. Depression, anxiety, apathy, agitation, or aggression may surface when needs go unmet or confusion becomes overwhelming. Wandering is common, as are disrupted sleep, paranoia, or hallucinations.

These manifestations are not random: they are messages. A person may lash out not because of their disease but because of untreated pain, hunger, overstimulation, or fear. Suppressing the behavior without addressing its cause risks stripping the person's dignity and increasing distress.

The most effective responses are rooted in detective work, which itself is rooted in observation of the person's daily life: adjusting the environment, building predictable routines, offering reassurance, and using simple communication strategies.

A PERSON-CENTERED APPROACH

Dementia and Alzheimer's reshape the lives not only of individuals but also of entire families. Adult children may become caregivers to their parents. Spouses may find their roles reversed. Family systems strain under the weight of responsibility.

In the midst of this, the person remains. Their life history, achievements, preferences, and values do not vanish with cognitive decline.

A person-centered approach emphasizes preserving identity by, for example, playing their favorite music, honoring food preferences, encouraging meaningful activities, and remembering the roles that shaped their lives. The goal is to see the whole person, not just the disease.

SUPPORTIVE ENVIRONMENTS

The environment shapes experience. Physical spaces should be safe but familiar, free of hazards, and structured with cues that aid navigation. For those with memory concerns, stability thrives when caregivers are consistent, routines are predictable, and activities are meaningful. Calm spaces, reduced noise, and sensory balance ease confusion.

These details protect dignity by creating surroundings where individuals can succeed instead of struggle.

COMMUNICATING THROUGH CHANGE

Communication must adapt as abilities change. Using simple words, one idea at a time, repetition, and positive framing make conversation easier. Non-verbal communication—touch, tone, and facial expression—becomes vital when words fail.

Photos, music, art, and spiritual practices can bridge gaps that spoken language no longer can. The goal is connection, not correction.

HEALTH, LEGAL, AND FINANCIAL CONSIDERATIONS

Medical care should be comprehensive and cautious. Some medications may slow decline modestly, but behavioral medications must be used sparingly because of their side effects. Regular reviews, advance planning, and coordinated providers are critical.

Legal and financial preparation should begin early while the person still has the capacity to participate. Durable powers of attorney, health care directives, wills, and trusts must be established or updated. Early planning reduces the likelihood of later guardianship battles and court involvement.

Asset protection strategies, Medicare and Medicaid planning, and regular financial reviews ensure that resources last and protect against exploitation.

The dementia journey typically unfolds in stages:

- **Early stages:** Focus on diagnosis, safety checks, and maintaining the individual's active role in planning for their future.

- **Middle stages:** Increased supervision and adapted routines become essential. Behavioral shifts, including sundowning, may emerge. Addressing sundowning requires structured schedules, calming evening routines, environmental adjustments, and sometimes medication.

- **Late stages:** Emphasis shifts toward comfort care, intensive physical support, and preparing families for end-of-life realities. Sundowning may still occur, but physical decline and communication loss often take center stage, requiring caregivers to focus on reassurance, presence, and physical care above all else.

At every stage, the priorities change, but the need for dignity, stabilization of symptoms, and intentional planning remains constant.

TECHNOLOGY AND INNOVATION

Technology is increasingly part of dementia and Alzheimer's care. GPS devices, medication reminders, and home monitoring systems enhance safety. Apps support caregivers with schedules, notes, and alerts.

Digital tools such as reminiscence therapy apps or cognitive stimulation games can be helpful. But technology should never replace the human presence that remains essential for emotional connection.

CULTURAL AND SPIRITUAL DIMENSIONS

Culture and spirituality shape how families understand dementia and make care decisions. Honoring traditions, family roles, and spiritual practices ensures that care feels respectful and rooted in meaning. Storytelling, legacy-sharing, and rituals allow the individual to remain connected to their identity even as abilities fade.

CASE STUDIES

HELEN: SUBTLE DECLINE AND GROWING RISK

Helen, an 82-year-old widow, had always prided herself on managing her checkbook with precision. Her trustee received neat quarterly reports and saw no reason for concern. But over the course of a year, small changes appeared. Helen missed payments on utility bills, misplaced her bank card, and called her advisor repeatedly with the same questions.

To her family, these quirks seemed harmless. On paper, she still appeared stable. But when a Life Care Expert visited, the reality was clear: the refrigerator was empty, expired medications filled the bathroom cabinet, and unopened mail covered the kitchen table. Helen was in the early stages of dementia. Without intervention, her independence and financial stability would quickly erode. What looked like order in her paperwork was unraveling in daily life.

ROSA: A JOURNEY WITH ALZHEIMER'S

Rosa, a retired teacher, was diagnosed with Alzheimer's at age 72. Once sharp and independent, she began forgetting names, became disoriented while driving, and showed signs of anxiety. Her husband Robert felt grief and was overwhelmed as he stepped into the role of caregiver.

A Life Care Expert joined their journey, shifting the family's approach from reactive to proactive. Photo albums with captions, music, and predictable routines helped Rosa stay connected. When she became agitated, Robert learned to comfort rather than correct her. Together, they created a structure that preserved Rosa's dignity while guiding critical decisions about driving, finances, and eventually residential care.

For professionals, Rosa's story demonstrates how coordinated input from medical, financial, legal, and care providers prevents families from being left behind by the pace of decline. With proactive oversight, Rosa's safety and resources were safeguarded. She experienced continuity and stability instead of crisis and loss.

KEY CONSIDERATIONS FOR PROFESSIONALS

As a fiduciary, attorney, or advisor, you are not expected to diagnose dementia or Alzheimer's. Your role is to remain aware that these conditions often appear gradually and can affect judgment and daily functioning long before families recognize it.

- **Notice red flags.** Unpaid bills, piles of unopened mail, or a caregiver speaking on behalf of a client may signal that more support is needed.

- **Encourage timely planning.** Key documents such as powers of attorney, health care directives, wills, and trusts should be reviewed while the client can still participate in decisions.

- **Support oversight.** Monitoring financial activity and ensuring proper documentation help protect both the client and the fiduciary role.

- **Engage expertise.** Life Care Experts can provide assessments and observations that reveal risks not visible in paperwork, helping families make informed choices.

You do not need to manage the care yourself. By recognizing when additional support may be valuable and guiding families to the right resources, however, you help safeguard dignity, stability, and long-term security.

The next chapter will turn to transitions into new living situations. While dementia often unfolds gradually, the need for change in care can arrive suddenly, destabilizing both the individual and their support systems. Understanding how to respond with structure and compassion is essential for protecting dignity and preventing escalation.

CHAPTER 14

SUPPORT IN TRANSITIONS TO NEW LIVING SITUATIONS

THE IMPORTANCE OF A WELL-COORDINATED TRANSITION

One of the most underestimated risk points in aging is the transition from hospital to home or into a senior living community. These moments are inherently destabilizing. For older adults who need more support than they can manage independently, hospitalization can be disorienting, humbling, and even dangerous. What often goes unnoticed are how vulnerable this period makes the individual and how easy it is for professionals, families, and even the clients themselves to miss the warning signs.

No one wants to feel like they are losing control, especially older adults who have spent decades managing households, raising children, and building careers. Accepting help with personal care or cognitive challenges is often perceived as weakness. So, they cover. They perform. They pretend things are fine when they are not.

UNDERSTANDING TRANSITIONS IN AGING

The aging process involves many types of transitions, each carrying risks if not addressed.

- **Health transitions** may follow a sudden event like a stroke, fall, or fracture, or they may reflect the gradual progression of chronic illnesses.

- **Cognitive transitions** alter how people make decisions, while sensory losses such as hearing or vision impairment erode safety and independence.

- **Functional transitions** appear when daily activities—walking, bathing, cooking, or managing medications—become harder. Home upkeep may fall behind, and adapting to new technology can feel overwhelming.

- **Social transitions** come with losses, whether of a spouse, of driving privileges, or of long-standing community roles. These changes often reduce connection and increase isolation.

- **Financial transitions** complicate care. Fixed incomes, rising costs, and the maze of benefit programs require families to make difficult trade-offs, often with incomplete information.

Every one of these shifts requires more than technical fixes. Each requires a framework of support that protects dignity and stability.

THE ROLE OF A LIFE CARE EXPERT

Without structured oversight, older adults risk medication errors, delayed follow-up, and avoidable complications. A Life Care Expert helps ensure smoother adjustments by preparing environments ahead of a move, coordinating medical care, and ensuring that new prescriptions, equipment, and therapies are in place. Frequent visits support adaptation, while ongoing coordination links physicians, therapists, staff, and families.

In care communities, Life Care Experts develop relationships with staff, building goodwill and ensuring the client receives attentive care. We do not just visit during business hours. We also show up early in the morning, late in the evening, or on weekends to verify consistency across shifts. These details matter because the quality of daily life often depends less on the physician's plan and more on how faithfully care is carried out.

CASE STUDY: LEROY'S NEW SEASON

Leroy was 85, a widower whose wife had passed away seven years earlier. Since her death, he had been living alone in a one-bedroom apartment. He managed as best he could, but the isolation was heavy, and his health began to decline.

One night, Leroy fell and struck his head. He was unable to get up. The next morning, a neighbor noticed his newspaper still outside and went to check on him. They found him on the floor with a serious head injury and blood nearby. Emergency services rushed him to the hospital.

Leroy's Power of Attorney (POA), who lived out of town, was immediately contacted. Recognizing that Leroy needed more support than his apartment could provide, the POA asked a Life Care Expert to see Leroy at the hospital. After the visit and evaluation by physical therapy they realized that returning Leroy home alone was no longer safe.

At first, Leroy resisted the idea of moving. He feared it would mean giving up his independence. The turning point came when the Life Care Expert began planning the transition with his POA. Instead of moving in Leroy with only a suitcase and a few boxes, they re-created a sense of home in his new living space. His favorite recliner was placed by the window, framed photos of his wife and children were hung in familiar arrangements, and his shelves were filled with well-loved books. Even the quilt his wife had made decades earlier was folded neatly at the foot of his bed, and his favorite mug waited in the kitchen cabinet.

When Leroy arrived at the assisted living community, he did not feel like he was entering an institution. He felt like he was stepping into "his" space. That sense of continuity gave him the confidence to embrace his new environment.

What happened next surprised everyone. Freed from the stress of managing daily life alone, Leroy began to thrive. He participated in activities, made friends, and developed a close relationship with another resident. They shared meals, attended programs, and found joy in each other's company. Leroy gained weight as well, not only because the food was better than his frozen meals at home but also because he was no longer eating alone.

For his POA, the relief was profound. Instead of feeling the constant burden of distance and uncertainty, he knew Leroy was safe and supported. For Leroy, the move became not the end of independence but the beginning of a new chapter filled with dignity, safety, and even unexpected love.

CREATING A COMFORTABLE AND SUPPORTIVE LIVING ENVIRONMENT

The emotional environment matters as much as the medical one. Too often, families move a loved one into a care setting with only a suitcase. This results in a situation that feels temporary, as though the person has been parked rather than settled.

As a Life Care Expert, I make sure the space feels like home. We bring in familiar furniture, arrange photos, stock favorite snacks, and pay attention to the details that communicate identity. Sometimes we even suggest wallpaper or artwork to create continuity with the client's previous home. These touches are not cosmetic: they are therapeutic. They remind the client that who they are still matters, that their story still has weight, and that this new chapter can hold comfort and familiarity.

Clients often reflect with me afterward that these details helped them embrace and even love their new home. What looks small on the surface becomes monumental in preserving dignity.

Transitions are not just about moving belongings from one place to another. They are about carrying forward a sense of identity, safety, and dignity into a new environment. With foresight and collaboration, what could feel like an ending can instead become a beginning, one where older adults thrive, families find relief, and professionals know they have safeguarded stability.

KEY CONSIDERATIONS FOR PROFESSIONALS

As a fiduciary, attorney, or advisor, your role is not to manage moves directly but to ensure they are structured and supported. Encourage families to involve a Life Care Expert early in the process, before hospital discharge or a crisis move forces decisions. Ask questions such as these:

- Has the environment been prepared for safety and comfort?
- Is the client's identity reflected in the new surroundings?
- Are medical, legal, and financial systems coordinated for the transition?

By framing transitions as both financial and human events, you demonstrate diligence, protect assets, and, most importantly, preserve dignity.

In the next chapter, we will consider what happens when rehabilitation and structured recovery after hospitalization are neglected. Too many older adults lose ground and, with it, their dignity, simply because timely recovery care was not pursued.

CHAPTER 15

REHABILITATION CARE AFTER HOSPITALIZATIONS

REHABILITATION AS A BRIDGE TO DIGNITY

Rehabilitation after illness, injury, or surgery is a crucial bridge between recovery and dignity for older adults. It helps individuals regain strength, mobility, cognitive function, and the ability to perform daily activities. Early rehabilitation improves outcomes, restores independence, and enhances quality of life. It also ensures that transitions, whether to a rehab facility, home, or assisted living, are safe and sustainable.

THE GOALS OF REHABILITATION AND TRANSITION SUPPORT

The goals of rehabilitation extend far beyond exercise. Rehabilitation is designed to restore physical strength and mobility, support cognitive recovery, and strengthen mental well-being. It works to prevent complications such as infections, falls, and muscle atrophy. It also facilitates safe transitions from hospital to the next care setting, enhances long-term health, and ensures that equipment, medication, and follow-up services are securely in place before discharge.

ACUTE REHABILITATION AND SKILLED REHABILITATION

Many older adults resist rehabilitation, fearing it will lead to permanent placement in a facility. In truth, rehabilitation is a temporary extension of hospitalization intended to protect independence.

Medicare covers two types of rehabilitation after a hospitalization of three days or longer:

- **Acute rehabilitation** involves at least three hours of therapy daily across disciplines such as physical, occupational, and speech therapy. It is usually recommended for major events like strokes, traumatic injuries, or complex surgeries and is delivered in specialized rehabilitation hospitals with daily physician oversight and a multidisciplinary team.

- **Skilled rehabilitation** offers moderate-intensity therapy, usually one hour a day, and is commonly provided in skilled nursing facilities. Physician rounds occur several times per week. Skilled rehab is appropriate for recovery from surgery, fractures, general debility, or chronic illness, with durations ranging from weeks to months depending on progress.

THE REHABILITATION MINDSET

Rehabilitation requires reframing expectations. The goal is not always full restoration but adaptation and optimization.

- Functional recovery means setting goals that matter to the individual, practicing tasks in real environments, and training for roles that preserve identity and purpose.
- Adaptive recovery involves compensation strategies, mobility aids, and home modifications that make life safer and more manageable.
- Preventive recovery emphasizes maintenance programs, risk reduction, and early detection of setbacks before they escalate.

COMPREHENSIVE REHABILITATION STRATEGIES

Rehabilitation spans multiple domains:

- Physical rehabilitation builds strength, endurance, balance, and mobility while managing pain and teaching safe movement.

- Occupational rehabilitation supports activities of daily living, such as bathing, dressing, cooking, and home safety, and integrates adaptive tools.
- Cognitive rehabilitation offers strategies for memory, attention, executive function, and problem solving.
- Speech and communication rehabilitation restores the ability to communicate, improves swallowing safety, strengthens voice, and leverages communication technologies.

MEDICARE COVERAGE

When eligibility criteria are met, Medicare covers both acute and skilled rehabilitation services following hospitalization. This includes physical, occupational, and speech therapy; skilled nursing; and physician oversight. After certain limits are reached, patients may face cost-sharing such as copays or coinsurance.

THE LIFE CARE EXPERT'S ROLE IN REHABILITATION

Life Care Experts ensure rehabilitation is supported at every stage. We facilitate communication between physicians, therapists, staff, and family so that care is coordinated and goals are clear. We also prepare for the post-rehabilitation phase by arranging outpatient therapy, home modifications, personal care services, and medical equipment.

Discharge planners sometimes skip critical steps, so we step in to ask for what we know is needed. We work directly with the discharge team to ensure that essential items such as walkers, hospital beds, or oxygen therapy are ordered and in place before the client returns home. When premature discharge is considered, we advocate for additional time if we know that more safety measures or in-home support is required.

THE HIDDEN COSTS OF POOR TRANSITIONS

One of the greatest threats to independence I see in my work is not aging itself but poor recovery after illness or injury. Even the best financial or legal plans fail when transitions are mismanaged. Too many older adults are discharged into homes that are unsafe, facilities that are understaffed, and communities that are unprepared to support them.

CASE STUDY: JAMES'S AVOIDABLE DECLINE

James was 82, widowed, and living alone in the home he and his wife had shared for more than forty years. After a winter hospitalization for pneumonia, his doctors recommended a short rehabilitation stay to rebuild strength and ensure that he could manage stairs, medications, and daily routines safely before returning home.

James refused. "I just want to be in my own bed," he told his daughter Frances. He associated rehabilitation with permanent nursing home care. Frances felt guilty and did not want to push him. The discharge planner, under pressure to free a bed, did not challenge the decision.

At home, James struggled immediately. He was weak and unsteady. His medication list had changed, and he was confused about timing and doses. Frances visited daily, but she worked full-time, had a family to care for, and could not stay overnight.

On his second night home, James stood up in the dark to use the bathroom. Without night lighting or grab bars, he lost his balance and fell. He fractured his hip and lay on the floor until morning, when Frances arrived.

The fracture required surgery and another hospitalization, followed by a much longer rehabilitation stay than he would have needed if he had accepted rehab after pneumonia. The setback was not just physical. The fall left James fearful and hesitant to move independently. He never regained his prior level of confidence or function.

A short, proactive rehabilitation stay could have provided targeted strengthening, medication review, and a safer transition home. Without that bridge, a preventable fall changed his quality of life permanently.

CASE STUDY: HAROLD'S CASCADE AND COURSE CORRECTION

Harold was 79, a retired math teacher who took pride in his evening walks and his careful diabetes management. A minor fall on his driveway left him with a hairline wrist fracture. The emergency department splinted it and sent him home with instructions to take it easy.

Taking it easy turned into spending most of the day sitting. Cooking with one hand felt overwhelming, so frozen meals replaced his healthy meals. His muscles weakened. His balance deteriorated. His blood sugar rose. Six months later, he tripped in the kitchen and broke his leg.

This time, his daughter Noel insisted on a different plan. A Life Care Expert coordinated discharge to home and then to acute rehabilitation, once his leg healed enough for weight bearing. The care included daily therapy, organized home safety modifications, and bringing in a dietitian to restore healthy routines.

Three months later, Harold was walking with a cane, back to his evening stroll, and once again in control of his diabetes.

The key difference was treating Harold's situation as a transition that required comprehensive support, not as an isolated medical event. The second fall was preventable.

The first recovery was incomplete because the transition was unmanaged.

RECOVERY DOES NOT END AT DISCHARGE

The greatest threat to independence is not age itself but incomplete recovery. Rehabilitation is not optional: it is the bridge between survival and dignity. James's decline and Harold's recovery illustrate opposite outcomes of the same lesson. Managed poorly, they fracture health and autonomy. Managed well, they strengthen foundations for the future.

KEY CONSIDERATIONS FOR PROFESSIONALS

Hospital discharge and rehabilitation are some of the most fragile phases in an older adult's life. Without structured oversight, these moments quickly become crises that drain resources, fracture families, and permanently diminish quality of life. For fiduciaries, attorneys, and financial professionals, recognizing that a hospitalization that requires rehabilitaton is not just a medical matter. It is a core planning responsibility.

Your role is to:

- Recognize that rehabilitation and recovery require structured oversight.
- Partner with Life Care Experts, which puts a focus on aligning recovery goals with financial and legal strategies.

- Encourage clients and families to see rehabilitation not as an institutional placement but as a temporary, protective bridge.

Recovery is about more than regaining function. It is about rebuilding confidence, protecting autonomy, and ensuring resources are used wisely to preserve dignity. The professionals who understand this are not simply reducing risk: they are safeguarding lives.

In the next chapter, we will examine the hidden crisis in aging and the critical role of oversight and intervention. While transitions represent one of the most visible gaps in the current system, deeper systemic failures continue to cause complicated concerns for the clients we serve.

CHAPTER 16

THE HIDDEN CRISIS IN AGING: WHY PROPER CARE IS CRITICAL

Beneath the surface of what appears to be normal aging lies a hidden crisis that few discuss openly: the preventable deaths and unnecessary suffering that occur when older adults fail to receive appropriate care and support. This crisis rarely makes headlines or sparks public outrage. Instead, it unfolds quietly in homes, hospitals, and care facilities across the country, claiming lives and compromising dignity in ways that could often be prevented with proper intervention and oversight.

The statistics are sobering, but they tell only part of the story. Numbers cannot convey the full cost of missed opportunities, delayed interventions, and care gaps that escalate manageable health concerns into life-threatening crises. In many cases, the root cause is not inadequate medical treatment but failures within the broader support systems that older adults depend on to remain safe and stable. These same failures expose families and professionals to both risk and sometimes liability.

THE SCOPE OF PREVENTABLE HEALTH CRISES

Medication-related deaths and injuries are among the most pressing risks. Older adults who take multiple prescriptions face exponentially higher chances of harmful drug interactions, side effects that mimic or mask other conditions, and medication errors that can prove fatal. Hundreds of thousands are hospitalized each year due to adverse drug events that could have been prevented with proper monitoring. Complex regimens often lead to confusion, missed doses, overdoses, or abrupt discontinuations.

Meanwhile, medications that are inappropriate for older adults continue to be prescribed, even when safer alternatives exist.

Falls are another leading cause of decline. They result in more injuries and hospitalizations than any other factor in older adults. A fractured hip is often the turning point, carrying a high one-year mortality rate because of the complications that follow. Head injuries, particularly for those on blood-thinning medications, can be devastating.

Even when falls do not cause catastrophic injury, the aftermath often triggers fear, reduced activity, and physical decline that accelerate frailty. Most of these incidents occur in homes that could have been made safer with simple modifications, yet those steps are often not taken until after crisis strikes.

Undiagnosed and untreated conditions add another layer of risk. Cardiovascular disease may present atypically in older adults, leading to delayed recognition and sudden cardiac death. Depression is often dismissed as normal aging, despite older adults having the highest suicide rates of any age group. Cognitive impairment frequently goes unrecognized, preventing families and professionals from putting support in place when it is most effective. Even minor infections can spiral into life-threatening events when symptoms are subtle and immune systems are weakened. A urinary tract infection may show up as confusion or behavioral changes, yet families often miss the signs until the situation has escalated.

Nutrition and hydration are also underestimated threats. Malnutrition weakens immune systems, slows wound healing, and accelerates frailty. Dehydration is common, driven by diminished thirst, medication side effects, and barriers to accessing fluids. Eating alone diminishes appetite, disrupting healthy routines, while social isolation compounds the problem. In some cases, disordered eating patterns emerge later in life, carrying significant health risks that families and professionals fail to recognize.

These examples demonstrate how easily stability unravels, even for clients with financial and legal planning in place.

Falls, untreated illnesses, medication mismanagement, and malnutrition are not anomalies. They are patterns we see repeatedly in the lives of the clients we support. Without structured oversight, serious health concerns go unrecognized until they escalate into crisis.

GENDER-SPECIFIC VULNERABILITIES

The hidden crisis in aging affects men and women differently, shaped by lifelong patterns of healthcare utilization, cultural expectations, and social supports.

Women often experience vulnerabilities tied to caregiver fatigue and financial insecurity. Many spent their lives caring for others while neglecting their own health needs. With longer lifespans and lower lifetime earnings, they face greater risk of poverty in old age. Widowhood and the loss of social networks create isolation, and women who have long advocated for others may struggle to advocate for themselves within a healthcare system that too often dismisses their concerns.

Men face a different set of risks. Cultural expectations of stoicism prevent many from seeking medical help until conditions are severe. Their social networks are often smaller, leaving fewer supports after retirement or spousal loss. Risk-taking behaviors combined with age-related vulnerabilities create added danger. And communication barriers, both cultural and personal, can prevent men from expressing health concerns clearly or seeking help when they need it most.

THE ROLE OF SOCIAL DETERMINANTS

Social determinants of health greatly influence whether older adults live safely, maintain independence, and access needed care. Housing is key. Multi-story homes become hazardous when mobility declines, unsafe neighborhoods discourage activity, and deferred maintenance creates daily risks. Transportation is another pivotal factor. Losing the ability to drive often triggers a downward spiral of isolation, depression, and decline. Public transportation is inadequate in many communities, particularly rural areas, and even when available may not be accessible for older adults with mobility challenges.

Economic insecurity compounds these risks. Fixed incomes make it difficult to keep up with medical bills, housing costs, and food expenses. High out-of-pocket healthcare costs lead many older adults to delay treatment or ration medications. Insurance gaps leave essential services uncovered. Financial exploitation strips away the very resources meant to preserve stability and dignity. Even those with considerable assets often fail to realize that what they saved should be used for their care, not left untouched while their quality of life deteriorates.

SYSTEMIC CONTRIBUTORS

The healthcare system itself often fuels the hidden crisis. Care is fragmented across multiple specialists with little coordination. Transitions from hospital to home or rehabilitation are poorly managed. Electronic health record systems fail to communicate, leaving dangerous information gaps.

Ageism also plays a role. Symptoms are dismissed as normal aging, leading to delayed diagnoses and missed treatments. Older adults may be excluded from interventions that could improve their health, or clinical protocols may not account for their needs. System incentives further perpetuate the problem, rewarding acute interventions over prevention or long-term care coordination. Families are assumed to be able to absorb caregiving responsibilities, even when they are unavailable or unprepared. These practices save money in the short term while creating far greater costs in the long term.

CASCADING EFFECTS

One of the most insidious aspects of the hidden crisis in aging is how small failures compound into larger cascades. A hospitalization can trigger delirium, deconditioning, and inappropriate medication changes that accelerate decline. Isolation after losing the ability to drive may lead to depression, cognitive deterioration, and neglect of self-care. Frailty builds gradually as inactivity, poor nutrition, and cognitive decline intersect, creating dependence without adequate support.

PREVENTION AND EARLY INTERVENTION

This crisis is not inevitable. Comprehensive assessments by Life Care Experts identify risks when they are still manageable. Regular medication reviews reduce inappropriate prescribing, simplify drug regimens, and monitor side effects. Home safety evaluations address hazards before falls occur. Strength training, vision and hearing support, and careful medication adjustments further reduce risks. Preventive screenings and vaccinations protect against escalating conditions. Nutritional support strengthens resilience. Mental health interventions reduce depression and suicide risk.

Families and communities play a vital role as well. Families must be taught to recognize warning signs and connect loved ones with resources before emergencies arise. Community programs provide connections, reduce isolation, and extend informal safety nets. Volunteer programs and emergency response networks add more layers of protection.

Professionals across disciplines must also step up. Primary care providers must integrate functional and social needs into medical care. Specialists must adapt their expertise to geriatric populations. Professionals and attorneys must include oversight of care in their planning strategies, not simply financial and legal protections.

When these layers of prevention and coordination are in place, the hidden crisis in aging transforms into stability.

Rather than cascading into decline, older adults are supported in ways that preserve identity, protect dignity, and sustain quality of life.

The hidden crisis in aging is not inevitable. With proper assessment, intervention, and oversight, most preventable deaths and unnecessary suffering can be avoided. There must be a shift from crisis response to prevention, from fragmented services to coordinated support, and from ageist assumptions to age-appropriate care. The goal is not to eliminate all risks but to ensure that older adults have the comprehensive support necessary to age safely and with dignity. Prevention saves lives, preserves assets, and strengthens the fabric of families and communities alike.

KEY CONSIDERATIONS FOR PROFESSIONALS

Inadequate or inconsistent care often leads to preventable crises that drain families and destabilize resources. Proper care functions as a fiduciary safeguard, protecting assets and dignity simultaneously. Partnering with Life Care Experts ensures that needs are monitored, warning signs are identified, and interventions occur before small issues escalate. Documenting these strategies as part of fiduciary oversight demonstrates prudence, reduces liability, and ensures client well-being.

The hidden crisis in aging is not written in the stars. It is written in the gaps between what professionals know and what they do. Closing those gaps transforms care from reactive crisis management into proactive prevention, making dignity the foundation of aging. Professionals who guide transitions with foresight create stability that honors identity while protecting long-term wellbeing.

As we move into Part Three, the focus shifts from systemic concerns in aging to the reality of supporting adults with complex needs. These are the individuals whose lives sit most precariously on the edge of crisis, and whose survival and dignity depend on the systems we build around them.

PART THREE

SUPPORTING ADULTS WITH COMPLEX NEEDS

Adults living with mental illness, addiction, trauma,or disability require more than transactions—they need coordinated, proactive support. This part examines the risks of fragmentation and highlights how stability can only come when professionals bridge legal, financial, and care systems. Here, proactive strategies become a lifeline for dignity and long-term sustainability.

The case studies in this section are composite examples. They are drawn from patterns observed in practice, with details anonymized to protect identities while illustrating key themes.

CHAPTER 17

EMPOWERING ADULTS WITH COMPLEX NEEDS: A JOURNEY OF DIGNITY, STABILITY, AND CARE

The landscape of adult disability has undergone a dramatic transformation over the past several decades. The focus has shifted from institutional models built around custodial care to community-based approaches that emphasize independence, choice, and participation in society. For many adults with complex needs, whether arising from developmental disabilities, acquired disabilities, mental health conditions, or combinations of multiple challenges, the promise of community inclusion remains only partially realized.

DEFINING COMPLEX NEEDS

DEVELOPMENTAL DISABILITIES

This group includes intellectual disability, autism spectrum disorder, cerebral palsy, and combinations of intellectual, physical, sensory, or behavioral challenges. Intellectual disability affects learning, reasoning, problem solving, and adaptive behavior. Autism affects communication, social interaction, and behavior in ways that require ongoing support. Cerebral palsy often brings with it both physical and cognitive needs. When multiple disabilities coexist, support needs become particularly complex.

ACQUIRED DISABILITIES

Acquired conditions include traumatic brain injury that alters cognitive, physical, or behavioral functioning after normal development and spinal cord injury that reduces mobility and independence while requiring environmental adaptations. Progressive disorders such as multiple sclerosis, ALS, or Huntington's disease bring gradually changing support needs. Sensory impairments, including blindness and deafness, require specialized support and modifications.

MENTAL HEALTH CONDITIONS

Serious mental illness such as schizophrenia, bipolar disorder, and major depression can significantly affect daily functioning.

Personality disorders create challenges in relationships and daily life management. Trauma-related conditions, including post-traumatic stress disorder, shape behavior and coping. Dual diagnoses, where mental health conditions co-occur with intellectual disability or substance use, increase complexity. Persistent behavioral challenges may require specialized interventions and support strategies.

MULTIPLE AND COMPLEX CONDITIONS

Many adults live with medical complexity, and their multiple chronic conditions require ongoing management alongside disability support. Communication needs may require alternative communication methods or specialized support. Aging layered onto lifelong disabilities introduces new risks and changing demands.

These realities reinforce that comprehensive, coordinated, and reliable systems of support are essential.

THE EVOLUTION OF SUPPORT PHILOSOPHY

This evolution mirrors broader shifts in values and practice. Institutional living once emphasized control, routine, and custodial care. Deinstitutionalization moved many individuals into group homes where the normalization principle took root, allowing daily life that looked and felt more typical. Today, community integration remains central, with increasing respect for individual preferences and cultural values. Person-centered planning encourages goal setting and choice. Self-determination shapes supports around strengths and interests. Recovery-oriented approaches in mental health confirm that growth can occur alongside ongoing limitations. Inclusive employment, housing, and relationships define success by belonging, not by program compliance.

PRINCIPLES OF EFFECTIVE SUPPORT

The guiding principles are straightforward. Dignity and respect must be visible in daily routines and decision making. Autonomy should be honored even when others perceive risk. Self-determination means the person's goals drive the plan. Inclusion places work, learning, and social life in integrated settings. Outcomes that matter most are personal satisfaction and a sense of belonging, not system efficiency alone.

COMPREHENSIVE SUPPORT IN PRACTICE

Effective support is coordinated across daily living assistance, medication management, and health oversight to maintain stability. Accessible housing in a neighborhood keeps people connected rather than isolated. Employment, even part-time, provides income, purpose, and social engagement. Participation in faith communities, volunteer opportunities, recreation, and friendships both within and beyond the disability community strengthen resilience. Financial stability depends on careful benefits planning, special needs trusts when appropriate, and consistent coordination so one change in services does not unravel progress elsewhere.

A Life Care Expert helps to link waiver services (public programs) with these pieces to daily reality, aligning disability services, healthcare providers, housing, and financial protections so that no single gap brings the whole system of support crashing down.

LEGAL FRAMEWORKS AND RIGHTS PROTECTION

Civil rights protections such as provided by the Americans with Disabilities Act and the Fair Housing Act safeguard access to integrated housing, employment, and public life. Supported decision making and limited guardianship can preserve autonomy while providing guidance where needed. Healthcare rights ensure informed consent and access to treatment. These frameworks protect dignity, but they must be translated into practice. A Life Care Expert helps ensure that the rights on paper function in real life by coordinating with counsel, trustees, providers, and families.

TECHNOLOGY AND INNOVATION

Modern technology can increase independence without amplifying risk. Assistive technology supports communication and mobility. Smart-home devices add safety and medication reminders. Video calling maintains connection with families and professionals. When integrated into the plan and monitored, these tools reduce reliance on constant in-person supervision while maintaining autonomy.

CASE STUDY: MARCUS'S JOURNEY

Marcus's story illustrates both the progress made and the challenges that remain. Born with cerebral palsy, Marcus spent his early childhood in a large state institution before deinstitutionalization efforts in the 1980s moved him to a group home. A trust established by his great-uncle later allowed him to build greater independence. Now 59, Marcus lives in his own apartment with support services, works part-time at a local grocery store, and participates actively in his community. His life demonstrates the best of what is possible when comprehensive support systems function well.

Marcus's success did not happen automatically. It required years of advocacy, careful planning, and coordination across multiple service systems. His story highlights the ongoing vulnerability of adults with complex needs who must navigate systems that are fragmented, underfunded, and difficult to access. When support systems work, they can transform lives. When they fail, the consequences can be devastating. Supporting adults with complex needs requires moving beyond simplistic notions of independence to embrace interdependence, supported decision making, and community inclusion. These concepts honor individual autonomy and the reality that all humans need varying levels of support to thrive.

THE ROLE OF FAMILIES AND COMMUNITIES

Family involvement and community inclusion are often decisive factors in stability. Families can provide advocacy, financial planning, and emotional support. A community's open doors through inclusive employment, housing, recreation, and civic opportunities make a significant difference for this population. Public programs, community networks, and family members create stability for adults with complex needs, but these programs can be fragile. Staff turnover, funding cuts, shifts in services, and family illness can quickly destabilize progress. A Life Care Expert provides continuity through these changes and keeps the plan aligned when the environment shifts.

TOWARD DIGNITY, STABILITY, AND CARE

Adults with complex needs thrive when systems align and remain vulnerable when they do not. Success requires commitment to person-centered outcomes, inclusive communities, and accountability for quality. Empowerment does not mean eliminating support. It means ensuring that support enhances choice, dignity, and belonging.

KEY CONSIDERATIONS FOR PROFESSIONALS

Approach adults with complex needs as individuals who require stability, not just crisis intervention. Build care and financial structures that anticipate cycles of progress and challenge. Partner with Life Care Experts to coordinate public programs, medical, legal, and social supports for long-term sustainability. Document outcomes in terms of dignity and stability, not only compliance or service delivery.

Marcus's story is a reminder that empowerment is not about doing everything alone. It is about having the right support at the right time in ways that enhance independence and dignity. By weaving together professional expertise, family involvement, community inclusion, waiver support, and the oversight of a Life Care Expert, you can create systems that safeguard stability while opening pathways to belonging.

Many needs in adulthood are not rooted in physical disability alone. Neurodivergence, including autism, ADHD, and other developmental differences, also shapes planning.

In the next chapter, we will explore how embracing neurodivergence reframes both support and opportunity, ensuring that unique minds are not only accommodated but also valued.

CHAPTER 18

UNDERSTANDING AND SUPPORTING UNIQUE MINDS

Neurodivergence is not a niche concern or a rare exception. It is a reality shaping the lives of millions of adults and families. Yet our systems of education, healthcare, law, and finance were not built with these individuals in mind. Too often, neurodivergent adults are forced to adapt to environments that misunderstand them, minimize their strengths, or leave them unsupported until a crisis makes their needs impossible to ignore.

This chapter challenges us to adopt a new perspective: one where neurological differences are not pathologized but are recognized as part of human diversity and where structures are intentionally designed to foster stability, independence, and dignity. By reframing how we see and support neurodivergent adults, professionals can help transform lives not by trying to change who they are but by changing the systems that do not serve them.

WHAT IS NEURODIVERGENCE?

Neurodivergence refers to variations in brain function that affect how individuals think, learn, process information, and interact with the world. Common neurodivergent profiles include giftedness, autism spectrum disorder, attention-deficit hyperactivity disorder, dyslexia and other learning differences, sensory-processing differences, Tourette syndrome and tic disorders, obsessive compulsive patterns, nonverbal learning differences, and trauma-related neurodivergence, such as the cognitive effects of post-traumatic stress. Rather than viewing these differences as deficits, the neurodiversity framework understands them as natural variations in human cognition.

Despite real challenges, many neurodivergent adults also have significant strengths when those strengths are noticed and supported. Deep focus and passion can lead to mastery, meaningful work, and personal fulfillment while building executive function over time. Creative problem solving often emerges in nonlinear thinkers, which, when paired with simple structures and consistent habits, becomes a powerful asset. Living in a world not designed for their cognitive style also builds resilience and adaptability, which can translate into leadership strengths. Heightened empathy and perception, when guided, can support relationship building, self-advocacy, and community engagement. When these strengths are acknowledged and paired with structure, accountability, and compassion, they become the foundation for a thriving life.

Life Care Experts help build that scaffolding, bridging the gap between potential and daily application in systems that too often default to seeing neurodivergence as limitation rather than capacity.

THE HIDDEN POPULATION: UNDIAGNOSED ADULTS AND THE STRUGGLE FOR SUPPORT

Awareness of neurodivergence has grown, but few neurodivergent adults, especially those older than their mid-twenties, were diagnosed in childhood. Traits were dismissed as personality quirks, behavior problems, or a lack of effort. As a result, many spent years struggling without context, improvising strategies while wondering why daily life felt harder for them than it seemed for peers. Their families often stepped in to manage finances, routines, and executive tasks. As parents age and can no longer provide support, these adults are left without skills, structures, or eligibility for programs that depend on a formal diagnosis.

WHY A DIAGNOSIS MATTERS FOR LONG-TERM PLANNING

A diagnosis in adulthood can provide context and open access to protections and services. It can enable legal and financial structures like a supplemental needs trust to support stability for those who struggle to manage independently. Most importantly, a diagnosis can provide a framework based on best practices and waiver services so that when family support changes, continuity of care does not depend on a crisis.

PLANNING FOR NEURODIVERGENT ADULTS

A formal diagnosis allows professionals and families to plan with purpose. Daily living tasks such as meals, hygiene, budgeting, and transportation often require structured assistance that is simple and consistent. As a Life Care Expert, we help our clients set up neuropsychological assessments to obtain a diagnosis, assess the home, identify barriers, connect to resources, and ensure that support is sustainable rather than episodic.

When employment or fully independent housing is not an option, benefits like SSI and SSDI and housing vouchers can form the person's financial base. Options range from group homes with 24-hour supervision to supported living with periodic check-ins to cohousing communities designed for peer support. Each works best when tied to ongoing professional oversight so daily realities remain aligned with long-range plans.

Medical care also benefits from coordination. With professional support, individuals can access routine healthcare, receive help during hospitalizations, and manage ongoing conditions in ways that reduce avoidable crises and preserve dignity. Financial security matters as well. A special needs trust can fund housing, education, healthcare, transportation, and oversight without jeopardizing benefits. Where executive function is limited, POA, guardianship, or supported decision making may be appropriate so trusted people can assist with finances, healthcare, and legal matters while respecting the individual's autonomy and voice. Together, these tools create a safety net that protects both independence and stability and outlasts the caregiving years of parents.

ADVOCATING FOR A MORE INCLUSIVE FUTURE

For many adults, the barrier is not identity but access. Adults seeking answers later in life often struggle to find professionals willing or able to evaluate neurodivergence. Expanding training for medical, mental health, and social service providers is essential, so adults are not overlooked because their presentation differs from childhood patterns.

Inclusion must also extend beyond healthcare. Employers can reduce barriers through clear communication, sensory-aware spaces, flexible schedules, remote roles, and job coaching. Housing programs, transportation systems, and community initiatives should adapt to accommodate, rather than exclude. Just as importantly, the narrative around diagnosis should shift toward acceptance and community, so diagnosis becomes a tool for support and stability, not a label of limitation.

CASE STUDY: PLANNING A LIFE BEYOND PARENTS

Max, a 23-year-old man with high-functioning autism, had long relied on both parents. His mother provided structure and advocacy. His father Walter, then age 72, supported him in quieter but essential ways. When his mother died suddenly, Max's world changed. Walter was grieving while also becoming the sole planner for Max's future.

Working with the family's attorney, Walter established a special needs trust using Max's inheritance. The attorney brought in a team early, including a vocational specialist, a mental health professional, and a Life Care Expert. At the time, Max was not employed and had few connections outside the home, even though he had a strong memory, a quick sense of humor, and deep passions. A vocational assessment identified roles that matched his temperament and abilities. Max secured a part-time position at a local library, a quiet and structured environment that fit him well. He joined a weekly art class and a peer group for neurodivergent adults, forming friendships and gaining a sense of belonging.

The Life Care Expert coordinated support with his waiver providers, so routines matched goals and Walter was not left to navigate alone. By the time Walter considered moving to assisted living, planning for Max's next chapter was already underway. With the care team, a group home near Walter's new residence was identified, allowing Max to live with independence and waiver support and to see his father regularly.

With SSI in place and the trust providing supplemental support, housing and services were secure. The Life Care Expert remained involved, visiting twice a month to coordinate services, adjust plans, and monitor needs. When Max became eligible for SSDI, the same coordination ensured a smooth transition.

For Max, this meant stability, structure, and growth. For Walter, it meant relief from carrying the future alone. **For professionals, it demonstrates how coordinated planning, legal structures, and ongoing oversight can align resources to protect independence, reduce long-term risk, and safeguard quality of life.**

KEY CONSIDERATIONS FOR PROFESSIONALS

Recognize neurodivergence as a different way of processing and engaging with the world. Adjust fiduciary, legal, and financial planning so supports align with how the individual actually thinks, communicates, and functions. Partner with Life Care Experts so accommodations extend into lived support, not just paperwork. Document strategies that honor strengths, reduce barriers, and promote dignity so oversight is proactive and inclusive.

What if we thought of difference not as a deficit? This chapter invites professionals to see neurodivergence not as a problem to fix but as an aspect of human diversity to notice and integrate into planning. When strengths are recognized and simple structures are built around them, we create lives of stability, dignity, and contribution for people whose value has too often been overlooked. For professionals, recognizing neurodiversity in planning reduces risk and ensures that support matches the individual, rather than forcing them into systems that fail.

In the next chapter, we carry this perspective into the realm of mental health. Just as neurodivergence requires recognition and structure, rather than correction, mental health crises require compassion, legal and clinical tools, and proactive planning. We will examine how fiduciaries, attorneys, and Life Care Experts can build systems that reduce escalation, protect dignity, and preserve stability in moments of profound vulnerability.

CHAPTER 19

NAVIGATING MENTAL HEALTH CRISES: A COMPASSIONATE APPROACH TO CARE AND LEGAL SUPPORT

THE HUMAN SIDE OF CRISIS

As a mental health professional and with personal family experience shaping my perspective, I have seen how mental health crises test both autonomy and dignity. A psychiatric emergency is never just a medical event: it is an experience that collides with law, human rights, and social systems. It challenges our assumptions about autonomy, identity, and dignity. Clinical and bureaucratic responses have their place, but they often do not reflect human reality. An effective response must do more than stabilize symptoms. It must preserve dignity, protect self-determination where possible, and keep the door open to recovery.

DIAGNOSES THAT OFTEN LEAD TO EMERGENCY EVALUATION

While any psychiatric diagnosis can destabilize, some are more commonly tied to emergency holds when paired with dangerous conduct or inability to care for self. These include schizophrenia and schizoaffective disorder with psychosis, bipolar disorder with mania, major depression with suicidal intent, delusional disorder with escalating risk, postpartum psychosis, severe PTSD with dissociation, and substance-induced psychosis when combined with a serious mental illness.

Personality disorders by themselves rarely meet the criteria for involuntary commitment. They are enduring patterns of behavior and perception, rather than acute medical conditions. However, crises involving personality disorders sometimes lead to hospitalization, either voluntary or involuntary, when acute risk is present.

For example, borderline personality disorder often presents with suicidal threats or self-harm that result in emergency admission. Antisocial personality disorder may intersect with the criminal justice system rather than psychiatry. Narcissistic personality disorder can destabilize into suicidality or psychotic-like symptoms under severe stress. Other personality disorders generally only lead to hospitalization when they overlap with mood disorders, psychosis, or acute suicidality.

Importantly, substance use disorder or dementia alone rarely meets the legal threshold. Dangerousness must be tied to a diagnosable mental illness under state law.

THE COMMITMENT PROCESS ACROSS THE UNITED STATES

Every state has statutes that govern voluntary and involuntary treatment. Voluntary admission allows a person to consent to inpatient care. Emergency or short-term involuntary holds are authorized when someone presents an immediate risk to self or others or cannot meet basic needs due to mental illness. These holds usually last 72 to 120 hours and require physician evaluation within hours of admission. Court-ordered extensions permit longer treatment after a hearing.

The labels differ for involuntary holds. Pennsylvania uses "201" and "302," California has "5150," Florida the "Baker Act," and New York "Mental Hygiene Law 9.39." Yet, the principles are the same: protect the person and the public, and allow courts to extend treatment when risk is ongoing.

ASSISTED OUTPATIENT TREATMENT (AOT), MENTAL HEALTH COURT, AND THE MENTAL HEALTH POWER OF ATTORNEY

Some states authorize Assisted Outpatient Treatment (AOT), a civil court order requiring adherence to an outpatient plan when someone refuses care but remains at risk. Mental health courts, now operating in many jurisdictions, divert individuals from jail into treatment under judicial oversight. Both strategies acknowledge that stability requires accountability and structure, not just hospitalization.

A mental health power of attorney allows someone to designate a trusted agent to make psychiatric decisions during periods of incapacity. A thoughtful document provides direction for intervention, supports timely treatment, and protects dignity during instability.

THE ROLE OF SPECIAL NEEDS TRUSTS

Special Needs Trusts protect eligibility for Medicaid, which provides broader coverage for crisis services, intensive outpatient care, and targeted case management than private plans in many regions. With a trust in place, essentials such as housing, transportation, and oversight can be secured without jeopardizing benefits. Estate planning that includes these trusts ensures individuals receive consistent care.

MEDICATION MANAGEMENT THAT CHANGES OUTCOMES

Medication adherence is often the difference between recovery and relapse. Long-acting injectables reduce the risk of noncompliance when insight is limited, and they should be initiated before discharge. Discharge planning must include follow-up appointments, clear medication schedules, and practical supports such as blister packs, transportation, or visiting nurse oversight. Without these, the cycle of relapse repeats.

THE VALUE OF A LIFE CARE EXPERT

Life Care Experts bring coordination and advocacy to psychiatric crises. We know which hospitals provide which services, how county systems operate, and when to escalate. We push for long-acting medication when adherence is poor, align legal protections with treatment teams, and ensure that courts, clinics, and professionals work together. Without that bridge, clients often cycle endlessly through ERs, jails, and shelters.

CASE STUDY: AMANDA'S JOURNEY WITH SEVERE MENTAL HEALTH

Amanda was 60 and living with schizoaffective disorder. Her history included homelessness, repeated hospitalizations, and legal involvement. A Life Care Expert was brought in when her family could no longer manage her care. At first, trust was nearly impossible. Through persistence and consistency, however, the connection grew.

At one point, Amanda was hospitalized involuntarily. The Life Care Expert pushed for long-acting injectables to be prescribed before discharge, knowing Amanda's history of nonadherence. The request was denied. Without that protection, she stopped taking her medication, lost her housing, and cycled back through crisis and jail.

Eventually, the Life Care Expert advocated for Mental Health Court involvement. With judicial oversight, stable housing, and injectables in place, Amanda's life was transformed. For more than three years she has lived independently, attending appointments, managing her health, and remaining engaged in her community.

Amanda's story demonstrates both the risks of fragmented care and the stability that emerges when legal, medical, and fiduciary systems align.

KEY CONSIDERATIONS FOR PROFESSIONALS

Mental health crises are not rare. They are a predictable part of fiduciary, legal, and financial practice. To meet this responsibility, professionals must:

- Incorporate mental health into intake conversations and planning.
- Ensure clients have a mental health power of attorney.
- Use Special Needs Trusts to preserve Medicaid access.
- Advocate for long-acting injectables when adherence is uncertain.
- Partner with Life Care Experts to bridge legal, medical, and practical supports.

When these elements are in place, a psychiatric crisis does not have to mean permanent decline. It can instead become a turning point toward recovery and dignity.

As a professional, you will encounter clients whose mental health directly affects their financial and legal stability. These are not just medical situations: they are systemic challenges that require planning, structure, and compassion. By building proactive support, you reduce liability, preserve resources, and safeguard dignity.

Not every mental health condition will result in hospitalization. Some unfold quietly, creating hazards that erode stability long before crisis intervention is required. A hoarding disorder is one of these conditions. It rarely leads to psychiatric admission, yet it can create life-threatening risks, legal entanglements, and family estrangement.

In the next chapter, we will reframe hoarding not as a moral failure but as a mental health condition requiring systemic understanding, legal awareness, and interdisciplinary intervention.

CHAPTER 20

HOARDING DISORDER: UNRAVELING THE COMPLEX HUMAN STORY BEHIND CLUTTER

UNDERSTANDING THE DEEPER NARRATIVE

Few mental health conditions are as misunderstood or stigmatized as hoarding. What may look like the careless accumulation of objects is often a profound narrative of survival. Hoarding is not about laziness or poor housekeeping. It is about protection, control, and attempts to create order in a world that feels unstable.

For many individuals, possessions act as boundaries and memories. They represent safety, identity, and sometimes the last connection to lost relationships. Hoarding is not a moral failing. It is a diagnosable psychological condition with biological, emotional, and social roots.

KEY FEATURES OF HOARDING DISORDER

Professionals need a clear lens to identify and respond properly to hoarding behaviors. Common features include the compulsive acquisition of items regardless of value, intense emotional attachment to possessions, distress at the thought of discarding them, progressive social isolation, and environmental dysfunction that makes daily life unsafe.

Research suggests that between one-half to four-fifths of individuals with hoarding disorder have a family history of similar behavior, indicating a genetic link. It may overlap with obsessive-compulsive disorder or autism spectrum traits, but it is recognized as its own condition.

Hoarding often emerges after trauma, grief, or life disruption. Each object can become a symbolic anchor against loss. Depression, anxiety, and PTSD frequently co-occur. Dementia and other executive function impairments can present with similar symptoms, which is why accurate diagnosis is critical before intervention begins.

LEVELS OF SEVERITY

The National Study Group on Chronic Disorganization developed a five-level scale to communicate risk, design interventions, and guide fiduciary decision making:

- **Level 1 Low Risk:** Light clutter, exits usable, no sanitation issues
- **Level 2 Mild:** Clutter interferes with rooms, minor odors, or pests
- **Level 3 Moderate:** Several unusable rooms, hygiene issues, infestations, withdrawal from social contact
- **Level 4 High Risk:** Severe environmental compromise, strong odors, structural damage, possible animal hoarding
- **Level 5 Crisis:** Entire home uninhabitable; immediate health, safety, and legal risks

Understanding these levels helps professionals decide when to escalate, involve Adult Protective Services, or seek court authority if voluntary cooperation fails. A Life Care Expert trained in this area can provide guidance and clinical insight.

APPROACHING HOARDING WITH COMPASSION AND STRATEGY

Decluttering alone is ineffective and often harmful. Lasting progress requires trauma-informed interdisciplinary care that balances dignity and safety.

Effective strategies include:

- **Psychotherapy:** Cognitive behavioral therapy and dialectical behavior therapy address underlying beliefs tied to possessions and help build new coping skills. Therapy should treat grief and trauma directly, not just the clutter.

- **Harm Reduction:** Life Care Experts may begin by creating one safe pathway, clearing a single room, or removing biohazards. The first priority is immediate safety, not instant transformation.
- **Medication:** Treating co-occurring depression, anxiety, or OCD can reduce the intensity of hoarding behaviors.
- **Team-Based Intervention:** Attorneys, fiduciaries, guardians, and Life Care Experts must coordinate to avoid re-traumatization, legal missteps, or family conflict.

CASE STUDY: ELIZABETH

Elizabeth, a 55-year-old woman, lived in a deteriorating home; her hoarding was at Level 5 severity. Untreated for decades, she shared the house with five living cats and eight deceased cats stored in her freezer.

Her guardian and Life Care Expert resisted the urge to force an immediate cleanup. Instead, they focused on trust building. When Elizabeth's mother died, a Special Needs Trust was established to provide oversight and therapeutic support. In a powerful act of respect, the deceased cats were cremated and placed in a memorial room in her new home. This validated Elizabeth's grief while opening space for healing.

Today, Elizabeth lives safely in a trust-owned home, participates in therapy, and maintains stability through Medicaid and other public programs, with her Life Care Expert providing ongoing oversight.

KEY CONSIDERATIONS FOR PROFESSIONALS

For professionals and attorneys, hoarding is not primarily about property preservation. It is about dignity. Each item carries meaning, and every room tells a story. The professional responsibility is not to erase those stories but to help the individual create a safer next chapter.

Hoarding is not evidence of irresponsibility. It signals deeper need. With patience and structured support, even extreme cases can be stabilized.

Recognize hoarding as a trauma-linked mental health condition, not a lifestyle choice. Understand that it can also be a symptom of another illness. Approach every concern with empathy and a harm-reduction mindset rather than coercion. Partner with Life Care Experts to coordinate mental health care, fiduciary oversight, and legal strategy. Document interventions thoroughly to demonstrate fiduciary diligence and reduce liability.

Behind every cluttered home is a human story of loss, resilience, and survival. When professionals and attorneys shift from judgment to understanding, they can transform outcomes, protecting not only assets but also dignity. Professionals who invest in structured oversight prevent these quiet crises from spiraling into financial and human catastrophe.

Addiction presents a parallel challenge. Like hoarding, it is often hidden, stigmatized, and misunderstood until crisis makes it unavoidable. Families, trustees, and attorneys may first see its effects in financial instability, health emergencies, or fractured relationships. Just as hoarding requires empathy and structured intervention, addiction demands that professionals look past behavior to the underlying human struggle.

CHAPTER 21

NAVIGATING ADDICTION: A COMPASSIONATE APPROACH TO CARE AND LEGAL SUPPORT

ADDICTION AS A HUMAN STRUGGLE

Addiction is not merely a medical diagnosis. It is a profound human struggle that intersects with mental health, legal systems, financial stability, and the fundamental questions of autonomy and dignity. It reshapes identities, fractures families, and challenges societal assumptions about responsibility and redemption.

Addiction does not discriminate by class or education. It affects people at every level of wealth and professional achievement. Privilege may provide more treatment options, but it does not prevent dependency. In fact, professionals such as attorneys, physicians, and executives often face higher rates of substance use disorders due to chronic stress, performance expectations, and stigma around seeking help. Their secrecy delays intervention, deepening the crisis.

To truly support individuals facing addiction, we must move beyond punitive frameworks. Effective systems of care prioritize dignity, agency, accountability, and the possibility of long-term recovery.

ADDICTION AS CRISIS AND A CHRONIC CONDITION

Addiction crises, like mental health crises, represent moments of extreme vulnerability. They are not simply behavioral issues but also are reflections of medical, psychological, and social realities.

Substance use disorders frequently overlap with mental health diagnoses such as depression, anxiety, PTSD, and bipolar disorder. Many people use substances to self-medicate untreated conditions, which creates dual diagnoses that complicate treatment. Both conditions must be addressed together if recovery is to take place.

Recovery is rarely linear. Shame, stigma, and systemic barriers fuel relapse. Many individuals cycle through multiple attempts at recovery before achieving stability. This is not failure; it is the nature of a chronic condition. Like diabetes or hypertension, addiction requires ongoing care, with setbacks understood as part of the process, rather than proof of defeat.

THE CONTINUUM OF SERVICES

Communities across the United States now deploy crisis response teams and specialized addiction services that bridge healthcare, law enforcement, social services, and legal advocacy. These teams intervene during acute episodes, connect individuals to treatment, and begin the shift from punishment toward recovery.

Treatment itself exists on a continuum from inpatient detoxification, residential rehabilitation, outpatient therapy, peer recovery networks, and medication-assisted treatment. The goal extends beyond abstinence to rebuilding lives, restoring stability through healthcare, and providing vocational training, housing support, and community reintegration.

THE ROLE OF THE LIFE CARE EXPERT

Life Care Experts help families and professionals navigate this continuum. They coordinate treatment providers, advocate for effective medication plans, structure financial supports, and help families maintain healthy boundaries. Importantly, they ensure that financial resources sustain recovery rather than enable relapse, directing funds toward treatment, housing, and structured oversight.

VOCATIONAL RECOVERY AND FINANCIAL PROTECTION

Employment is central to long-term recovery. Gaps in work history, legal records, and loss of skills make finding work difficult. Vocational assessments, job coaching, and workplace advocacy give people a path forward. Even part-time work restores purpose and income, reinforcing stability.

Families often carry heavy financial burdens from the high costs of treatment, legal fees, and lost income. Attorneys, trustees, and Life Care Experts help manage this strain by building structures such as discretionary or substance use disorder trusts. These tools safeguard assets while ensuring funds support care, not addiction. Allowances can be structured around treatment engagement, with trustee oversight protecting both the family and the individual.

LEGAL AND ESTATE PLANNING TOOLS

Estate planning is essential when addiction is part of the family story. Specialized trusts ensure continuity of care while preventing financial exploitation. Their provisions may require treatment participation, limit direct access to cash, or grant trustees authority to control expenditures.

Other instruments, such as carefully tailored powers of attorney or guardianship provisions, can give trusted decision makers authority to initiate treatment admissions during crises or restrict financial decisions during active addiction. These are not technicalities: they are safeguards that preserve dignity and protect families during instability.

AN INTEGRATED APPROACH TO RECOVERY

An effective model of addiction support is interdisciplinary and trauma informed. It includes these elements:

- Trauma-informed care that addresses underlying experiences fueling substance use
- Medication-assisted treatment for opioid and alcohol dependence
- Peer support networks that provide accountability and encouragement
- Legal advocacy to manage criminal justice involvement, housing stability, and workplace protections
- Family therapy and education to rebuild trust and repair relationships
- Financial and estate planning to protect assets and ensure continuity of care
- Vocational supports to restore independence and purpose
- Oversight from Life Care Experts who integrate these pieces into a sustainable framework

CASE STUDY: BRUCE'S JOURNEY WITH OPIOID ADDICTION

Bruce was a 36-year-old father whose struggle with opioid addiction revealed the complexity of substance use disorders. Once a Division I athlete and successful entrepreneur, Bruce's life was derailed by a knee injury that led to prescribed opioids. What began as pain management evolved into dependency and then into full addiction.

His business partner took on increasing responsibility as Bruce's behavior grew erratic. His marriage ended in divorce, and custody of his children shifted to his ex-wife. Several DUI charges, cycles of outpatient treatment, and repeated relapses followed. After a near-fatal overdose, Bruce's parents, exhausted and fearful, engaged a professional trustee and a Life Care Expert to stabilize the situation.

The team coordinated a recovery strategy that included inpatient rehabilitation, structured financial oversight, and family counseling. The program was tailored to professionals like Bruce, offering both medical treatment and vocational reintegration.

Two years later, Bruce remains sober. He is active in aftercare, therapy, and peer support groups. He has begun to rebuild his role in the business. His relationship with his children has improved, and his co-parenting with his ex-wife has stabilized.

None of this was due to sheer willpower alone: it was the product of a structured, compassionate, and coordinated plan.

A CALL TO COMPASSIONATE PROFESSIONALISM

For fiduciaries, attorneys, and healthcare providers, addiction is not a matter of simply fixing a problem. It requires long-term planning, empathy, and disciplined structures. Effective support:

- Recognizes addiction as a medical condition rather than a moral failure.
- Balances harm reduction with accountability.
- Respects agency while ensuring safety.
- Builds networks of interdisciplinary support.

Recovery is not about perfection. It is about progress sustained over time. With the right plan, recovery is not only possible but is probable.

KEY CONSIDERATIONS FOR PROFESSIONALS

Understanding addiction as a chronic condition requires structured oversight, not a one-time intervention. Build plans that anticipate relapses and protect financial resources through legal and fiduciary safeguards. Partner with Life Care Experts who can coordinate providers, trustees, and legal systems. Document strategies carefully to enhance fiduciary diligence and demonstrate accountability. When professionals address addiction proactively, they protect not only the individual but also the stability of the care and financial plan.

What if recovery was never about erasing relapse, but about building resilience? Addiction reframed as a journey of dignity and stability opens the door for individuals and families to heal.

Catastrophic injury presents a different but equally profound disruption. In an instant, an accident, stroke, or traumatic brain injury can change the trajectory of independence, work, and family roles. Where addiction challenges our assumption that recovery is linear, catastrophic injury challenges assumptions about stability and capacity. Both require systems of care, legal planning, and financial structures that preserve dignity while building pathways forward.

CHAPTER 22

LIFE AFTER CATASTROPHIC INJURY: REBUILDING DIGNITY, INDEPENDENCE, AND SECURITY

UNDERSTANDING CATASTROPHIC INJURIES AND THEIR LONG-TERM IMPACTS

A catastrophic injury is more than a medical diagnosis. It is a permanent interruption in the course of a person's life. Injuries such as traumatic brain injury, spinal cord damage, limb loss, severe burns, or multi-organ trauma can change an individual's capacity for movement, thought, communication, and independence in an instant.

The ripple effect is extensive. Families are suddenly overwhelmed by medical needs, financial stress, and logistical complexity. Housing may need to be modified. Vehicles may require adaptation. Employment is often lost. Emotional stability is shaken.

Chronic pain, cognitive impairment, and personality or behavioral changes become part of daily life. The caregiver, often a spouse or parent, is left balancing compassion with exhaustion while managing the weight of decision making and coordination.

Catastrophic injuries require more than medical stabilization and legal settlements. They demand a coordinated, long-term strategy that addresses not only care and costs but also identity, dignity, and the reshaping of daily life. These services protect trusts and reduce liability by preventing destabilization, financial strain, and family conflict.

THE LIMITATIONS OF TRADITIONAL LIFE CARE PLAN COST PROJECTIONS

Life Care Plan cost projections are frequently introduced during litigation to estimate the long-term medical and personal care needs of individuals who have sustained catastrophic injuries. These projections are typically developed by medical or rehabilitation experts and used to calculate settlement values.

The problem is that most of these care plans are rarely implemented. Once legal proceedings are complete, the document is often filed away by attorneys or trustees and forgotten. Families are left with the burden of decision making and coordination, often without the clinical knowledge or system navigation skills to do so effectively.

Even more concerning: these projections often fail to capture the true cost of care. While they may look thorough, they are usually created by professionals who are not familiar with the day-to-day realities of caregiving or service delivery.

Without a Life Care Expert involved before the plan is finalized and after the case is settled, rarely does the promised support materialize. A Life Care Expert can identify when projections are unrealistic or outdated, adjust the plan as needs change, interpret clinical language, and coordinate the delivery of services in real life.

FINANCIAL STRUCTURES THAT SUPPORT LONG-TERM CARE

Legal and financial structures are essential to sustainability. Life Care Experts can collaborate with lawyers and financial advisors to ensure that settlement funds and trusts are managed with long-term care in mind.

Structured settlements are often central to this process. They provide a steady stream of tax-free income, rather than a single lump sum, offering predictability and protection against the premature depletion of assets.

When paired with a properly structured trust and a trustee supported by a Life Care Expert, these tools create long-term stability while preserving access to quality care.

THE IMPORTANCE OF PERIODIC REVIEW

The Life Care Plan created at the time of injury almost never meets the client's needs five or ten years later. Medical advances, the effects of aging, mental health changes, and new technologies often shift what is required.

Annual reassessment and professional input are therefore essential. Without this oversight, families are left to guess, and funding decisions often fail to align with actual outcomes.

A Life Care Expert or Life Care Manager ensures that the plan reflects current needs and that services are delivered effectively. This role protects trusts, stabilizes families, and ensures that care remains both practical and sustainable.

CASE STUDY: MARVIN'S STORY

Marvin was 56 when he sustained a traumatic brain injury in a work-related accident. The injury altered his ability to manage daily tasks, regulate his emotions, and live safely without support. He received a structured settlement and a formal Life Care Plan outlining projected needs for therapy, supervision, medical care, and housing adaptations.

At first, Marvin's wife Annelise tried to manage everything herself. She continued to work a demanding professional job while raising their teenage twin boys, who were preparing to graduate from high school. At home, she coordinated Marvin's appointments, medications, and care needs. But it quickly became clear that this was not sustainable.

The emotional, logistical, and cognitive demands were too great. The family was spiraling under the weight of unstructured responsibilities.

That is when a Life Care Expert was brought in to help implement Marvin's Life Care Plan and coordinate his transition into a therapeutic residential program for individuals with traumatic brain injuries. The facility provided around-the-clock care, structured therapy, and a predictable routine tailored to his specific needs. It provided the type of specialized care that is rarely accounted for in standard legal planning.

With professional oversight, Marvin's care plan was finally put into action. He stabilized both emotionally and cognitively. His therapies were adjusted over time based on his response and evolving needs.

Most importantly, his wife was no longer alone in trying to manage an impossible situation. She could return to her professional role and resume her place in the family as a spouse and parent, rather than as a caregiver trying to hold the entire system together. The twin boys were able to finish high school knowing their father was safe and their mother was supported.

Today, Marvin remains in his therapeutic living environment. He continues to receive care that respects his dignity and supports his progress. His family has structure and relief, and they visit daily. His settlement is no longer a static number in a legal document but an active tool supporting real care.

A catastrophic injury does not just happen to one person. It happens to the entire family. The path forward is rarely clear, but it becomes manageable with the right team, tools, and systems in place.

Marvin's story illustrates how coordination, proper legal and financial structures, and care management can turn a family's overwhelming crisis into a stable and functional life. His wife was able to return to her professional role and regain balance. His sons were able to move into adulthood with more security. And Marvin, though still living with significant challenges, has access to consistent care and a life of greater dignity and structure.

The goal in complex care is not perfection. It is sustainability. When legal settlements are matched with real-world planning and compassionate execution, families like Marvin's do not just survive: they begin to rebuild.

KEY CONSIDERATIONS FOR PROFESSIONALS

Recognize that catastrophic injuries create lifelong shifts that require coordinated legal, medical, and financial planning. Prioritize rehabilitation, adaptive technology, and home modifications as investments in dignity and long-term independence. Engage a Life Care Expert who can align medical providers, fiduciary oversight, and support services into a sustainable framework.

Document evolving care needs and financial strategies to ensure ongoing stability and protect against future crises.

What if the injury changes everything, but not the person? Dignity can be rebuilt when care is coordinated, futures are planned, and identity is honored. Safeguarding independence requires professionals to move beyond paperwork and into proactive, coordinated oversight

The same is true for living with a disability. In addition to medical recovery, individuals often face questions of purpose, financial stability, and independence. These are not just clinical or legal issues. They are matters of identity and belonging, which we turn to in the next chapter.

CHAPTER 23

FINDING PURPOSE IN DISABILITIES: EMPLOYMENT, FINANCIAL INDEPENDENCE, AND DISABILITY BENEFITS

EMPLOYMENT AS PURPOSE

Employment is more than a paycheck. For individuals with disabilities, it can be a source of identity, purpose, and connection to the wider world. Work provides structure, social interaction, and the pride that comes with contributing skills and talents to a community. Yet the path to sustainable employment and financial independence is complex, particularly when government benefits and long-term care needs must be preserved.

The ability to work while maintaining necessary benefits requires both legal understanding and a coordinated plan that addresses personal goals, medical needs, and financial stability. Employment, benefits, and planning must intersect in ways that support independence without jeopardizing essential resources.

ADA PROTECTIONS AND WORKPLACE ACCOMMODATIONS

The Americans with Disabilities Act (ADA provides critical protections for employees with disabilities, requiring employers with 15 or more employees to offer reasonable accommodations so individuals can perform essential job functions.

Accommodations may include the following:

- Modifying work schedules or allowing remote work.
- Providing assistive technologies such as screen readers or voice recognition software.
- Adjusting physical workspaces for accessibility.
- Offering job restructuring or modified duties.
- Providing interpreters, captioning, or written materials in accessible formats.

The law is clear, but barriers remain. Employers may lack training, or employees may not know what modifications they are entitled to request. Advocacy and partnership with supportive organizations bridge this gap, ensuring that legal protections translate into practical access.

VOCATIONAL REHABILITATION AND SUPPORTED EMPLOYMENT

State vocational rehabilitation programs prepare individuals with disabilities for employment and help them secure and maintain meaningful work. Services may include:

- Career counseling and job training.
- Workplace assessments and on-the-job coaching.
- Educational support and skill-building programs.
- Assistance in obtaining and using assistive technology.
- Job placement and retention services.

For those requiring more intensive support, supported employment programs provide job coaches who remain involved as long as necessary, ensuring that both employee and employer succeed.

The most effective approaches go beyond mere compliance. They create workplaces where inclusion is cultural, where contributions are valued, and where accommodations are seen as tools for success rather than burdens.

NAVIGATING DISABILITY BENEFITS

Several government programs provide critical financial and medical supports:

- **SSI (Supplemental Security Income):** Needs-based income support for those with limited resources. Savings are tightly restricted unless funds are sheltered in a Special Needs Trust or ABLE account.
- **SSDI (Social Security Disability Insurance):** Benefits for individuals who have paid into Social Security through payroll taxes. Eligibility depends on work history, not financial need.
- **Medicaid:** Health coverage for SSI recipients and, in some states, allows individuals with disabilities to work and retain coverage.

Concerns about losing benefits are real. Fortunately, Social Security work- incentive programs reduce those risks.

Trial Work Periods: allow SSDI recipients to work for a set time without losing benefits.

Social Security Ticket to Work: provides vocational services, rehabilitation, and ongoing employment support.

FINANCIAL PLANNING FOR LONG-TERM INDEPENDENCE

True independence requires careful planning to balance wages, benefits, and long-term care costs. Here are some essential tools:

- **Special Needs Trusts (SNTs)** protect assets while preserving benefit eligibility.
- **ABLE Accounts** are tax-advantaged savings accounts for disability-related expenses.
- **Structured Settlements** provide predictable, long-term income after litigation or injury.
- **Life Care Plans**, when implemented by a Life Care Expert, become living frameworks that adapt to ongoing needs.

The strongest plans integrate employment opportunities with benefits protection, ensuring that individuals gain both financial security and personal fulfillment.

CASE STUDY: MAYA'S JOURNEY TO STABILITY AND PURPOSE

Maya, a 28-year-old with cerebral palsy, lived at home and was dependent on Supplemental Security Income (SSI) and Medicaid. She wanted to work but feared losing the medical coverage she relied on for her complex health needs.

With support from her trustee and a Life Care Expert, Maya connected with a state vocational rehabilitation counselor who developed a structured plan. A job coach arranged adaptive equipment, educated her employer, and ensured a smooth transition. Maya also learned about Social Security work incentives such as the Trial Work Period and Ticket to Work, which allowed her to earn income without immediately losing benefits.

Today, Maya works part-time, contributes to her expenses, and saves in an ABLE account for long-term goals. She continues to receive Medicaid, but her work provides structure, pride, and a renewed sense of identity. **Her progress illustrates how trustees and Life Care Experts can strategically align fiduciary resources to preserve benefits while enhancing her long-term quality of life.**

KEY CONSIDERATIONS FOR PROFESSIONALS

Employment offers dignity, purpose, and identity, not just income. For attorneys, trustees, and financial professionals, the challenge is to design strategies that protect benefits while expanding opportunities. Financial planning must anticipate the interaction between wages, benefits, and trusts. Life Care Experts can provide guidance on waiver programs, vocational supports, and care oversight, ensuring that employment success does not come at the cost of medical stability or long-term financial security. Plans should be revisited regularly, because policies shift, health changes, and personal goals evolve.

When these elements are aligned, employment becomes more than a paycheck. It becomes a gateway to dignity, belonging, and long-term independence.

Stability at work and in life depends on something even more fundamental: access to healthcare that is competent, coordinated, and consistent. For many adults with disabilities, the medical system is fragmented, overwhelming, and intimidating. Insurance coverage may determine access to specialists. Discharge planning may fail without advocacy. Preventable crises can spiral when care is delayed or disconnected.

This is where the next challenge emerges: ensuring healthcare is not just available but also navigable. In the following chapter, we will explore how coordinated advocacy within the healthcare system protects dignity, strengthens independence, and enables sustainable, long-term stability even for those with complex medical needs.

Employment and financial independence are only part of the picture for adults with disabilities. To sustain dignity and stability, they also need strong advocacy within the healthcare system, the focus of the next chapter.

CHAPTER 24

HEALTHCARE ADVOCACY AND NAVIGATING THE MEDICAL SYSTEM

THE ESSENTIAL ROLE OF HEALTHCARE ADVOCACY

The healthcare system, despite its remarkable advances, can be a maze of complexity. For adults with disabilities, mental health diagnoses, or addiction, navigating care often requires specialized knowledge, persistent advocacy, and strategic planning that go far beyond typical patient capabilities. Healthcare advocacy is not optional. It is essential to ensure that individuals receive appropriate, respectful, and effective medical care.

UNDERSTANDING HEALTHCARE DISPARITIES

Adults with disabilities face barriers at every level of healthcare. Facilities may be inaccessible. Appointment structures often fail to allow adequate time for transfers, communication, or a thorough examination. Many providers are unfamiliar with adaptive equipment or disability-specific conditions. Communication barriers arise when clinicians are untrained in working with individuals who use alternative communication methods.

Equally harmful are attitudinal barriers. Some providers underestimate an individual's communication capacity, assume a diminished quality of life, or default to a paternalistic model that strips away decision-making authority. Too often, disability is seen only as pathology, rather than as part of human diversity. These attitudes compound knowledge gaps, leaving individuals misunderstood, misdiagnosed, and underserved.

ESSENTIAL COMPONENTS OF HEALTHCARE ADVOCACY

Advocacy operates at multiple levels. At the individual level, self-advocacy skills matter. Adults with disabilities benefit from understanding their health needs, knowing their rights under the Americans with Disabilities Act (ADA), and keeping accurate records of medical histories and medications. Clear communication of symptoms, concerns, and preferences is vital.

Yet self-advocacy alone is rarely enough. Professional support often makes the difference. Life Care Experts, benefits advocates, and legal advisors bring specialized knowledge of systems, coverage rules, and patient rights. Family members and peers also play a role by offering support, encouragement, and systemic pressure for improvement.

PREPARING FOR HEALTHCARE ENCOUNTERS

Effective advocacy begins long before a medical visit. Maintaining thorough health records, medication lists, and emergency contacts allows for efficient and accurate care. Preparation for visits means arranging accommodation, clarifying communication needs, and identifying trusted supporters who can attend appointments. It also means knowing one's rights and being ready to request interpreters, extended appointment times, or accessible formats.

BUILDING PROVIDER RELATIONSHIPS

Strong provider relationships are the foundation of effective healthcare. Choosing clinicians with disability experience, evaluating facilities for accessibility, and seeking respectful communication styles create the conditions for trust. Once established, these relationships are strengthened by clear communication, healthy boundaries, and feedback that encourages improvement.

Ongoing communication is equally critical. Regular updates to primary care providers, coordination across specialists, and proactive sharing of changes in health status foster continuity. Emergency planning should be addressed in advance, so crises do not lead to fragmented or unsafe care.

NAVIGATING EMERGENCY HEALTHCARE

Emergencies require special preparation. Portable health records, identification of the preferred hospital, and plans for managing medical equipment improve safety. In the emergency department, quick communication of needs, informed consent supported by tools, and accurate pain assessment can change outcomes. During hospital stays, advocacy ensures accessibility, protects personal devices, and secures proper attention to care and communication needs.

PREVENTIVE HEALTHCARE ADVOCACY

Preventive care is often overlooked in adults with disabilities, but it is vital. Advocacy ensures access to standard screenings, as well as to disability-specific services such as bone density checks, cardiovascular monitoring, reproductive healthcare, and pressure ulcer prevention. Mental health screening should be integrated into every care plan.

MANAGING COMPLEX MEDICAL CONDITIONS

Complex needs require coordination across multiple providers. Advocacy aligns treatments, prevents conflicts, and ensures providers work toward shared goals. Medication management is a critical part of this process. Regular reviews, monitoring for side effects, and supporting adherence while respecting autonomy protect both safety and independence.

Treatment decisions must be accessible. Risks and benefits should be explained in context, options should be fully explored, and choices should reflect individual goals and values, not just clinical efficiency.

INSURANCE AND HEALTHCARE COVERAGE

Coverage systems create another layer of challenge. Advocacy helps navigate prior authorizations, appeals, and coverage gaps while ensuring that providers supply the necessary documentation. Medicaid and Medicare navigation requires knowledge of waiver programs, durable medical equipment coverage, and dual eligibility rules. Navigating private insurance demands equal persistence to challenge discriminatory practices, secure qualified providers, and enforce accommodation rights.

TECHNOLOGY AND HEALTHCARE ACCESS

Assistive technology is reshaping care. Communication devices, medical alerts, and medication management systems can dramatically improve safety and independence when properly implemented. Telehealth expands access to specialists and mental health services but still faces challenges, such as limited internet access, inaccessible platforms, and privacy concerns. Advocacy ensures that technology fulfills its promise rather than becoming another barrier.

SYSTEMIC HEALTHCARE ADVOCACY

Beyond individual care, systemic advocacy is necessary. Policy reform must strengthen accessibility standards, expand provider training, and integrate disability content into medical education. Communities contribute by developing disability-friendly resources, recruiting skilled providers, improving accessibility, and launching awareness initiatives.

CASE STUDY: MARIA'S STORY

Maria was born with spina bifida. Through childhood and young adulthood, she became adept at managing her own care. At age 29, she moved to a new city for employment and encountered a healthcare system unprepared for her needs. Emergency room staff were unfamiliar with her condition. Her new physician dismissed recurring urinary tract infections as "typical." Specialists seemed more focused on her wheelchair than on her symptoms. Without effective advocacy, Maria's health declined, her work suffered, and her confidence in the healthcare system collapsed.

When her trustee engaged a Life Care Expert, her experience shifted dramatically. Together they developed strategies for self-advocacy and prepared systems for appointments. She researched providers in advance, requested accommodation, and brought support to key visits. With this structure, Maria connected with providers willing to learn about her condition and collaborate. Her infections were correctly diagnosed and treated, and she built a comprehensive prevention plan with her team. Most importantly, she regained confidence and began mentoring younger adults with spina bifida.

Maria's story highlights both the disparities individuals face and the transformative impact of structured advocacy.

KEY CONSIDERATIONS FOR PROFESSIONALS

Every trustee carries responsibility not only for assets but also for the person at the center of the trust. If they are unaware of functional and medical realities, attorneys, trustees, and financial advisors may unknowingly fail to safeguard well-being. This can lead to conflict, family disputes, or even litigation. Partnering with a Life Care Expert creates documented oversight, clear accountability, a measurable standard for quality of life, and a defensible process. It demonstrates diligence by showing that decisions considered both financial stewardship and human needs.

Healthcare advocacy is not about being difficult. It is about being heard, respected, and treated with the same dignity every patient deserves. Advocacy transforms healthcare from a system that passively accommodates disability into one that truly serves people. Professionals should:

- Recognize that navigating healthcare is often overwhelming, especially for individuals with complex needs.
- Build fiduciary and legal plans that include proactive healthcare advocacy as part of protecting best interests.
- Engage a Life Care Expert who can attend appointments, coordinate providers, and translate medical information into actionable strategies.
- Document healthcare decisions and advocacy efforts to ensure accountability, reduce liability, and protect both client well-being and trust resources.

The same principles become even more urgent when the patient is a child. Families raising children with special needs face not only medical complexities but also educational hurdles, financial strain, and the lifelong challenge of planning for continuity of care. The stakes are higher, the systems more fragmented, and the need for advocacy even more profound.

PART FOUR

SUPPORTING CHILDREN WITH SPECIAL NEEDS

Families of children with disabilities face unique pressures that require more than just preparing planning documents or financial projections. This part demonstrates how proactive systems protect not only the child but also the caregiver's capacity to sustain support over time. By bridging professional insight into family needs, dignity can be safeguarded from childhood into adulthood.

This section explores that journey. It begins with holistic family support, then addresses educational advocacy, and finally navigates the transition to adulthood.

The stories in this part are composite case studies, anonymized to protect the dignity and privacy of children and families.

CHAPTER 25

SUPPORTING FAMILIES OF CHILDREN WITH SPECIAL NEEDS

THE FAMILY JOURNEY

Families raising children with special needs walk a path filled with complexity, resilience, and profound love. From the moment of diagnosis, whether at birth or later in childhood, every decision about healthcare, education, financial security, and daily living carries long-term impact. Parents and guardians are their child's fiercest advocates, but the weight of navigating fragmented systems often leads to exhaustion. What makes a difference is when professionals walk alongside caregivers, providing structured, multidisciplinary support that connects the dots across medical, legal, financial, and educational domains.

BUILDING A FOUNDATION OF SUPPORT

The first step is ensuring families understand their rights and available resources. Medicaid waivers, early intervention programs, and community-based supports can dramatically improve a child's quality of life. Yet eligibility rules and application processes are complex, and families often miss out on critical benefits. Life Care Experts provide guidance through this maze, ensuring that no opportunity for stability is lost.

Equally important is legal and financial planning for long-term security. Special Needs Trusts and ABLE accounts protect eligibility for government benefits while creating a means to cover essential expenses, such as therapies, education, and housing. Trustees, financial planners, and attorneys who collaborate with Life Care Experts reduce risk, prevent family conflict, and create structures that carry forward when parents can no longer provide direct care. Estate planning considerations, such as naming guardians and outlining future caregiving arrangements, ensure continuity across the child's lifespan.

EDUCATION: THE ARENA OF FIRST ADVOCACY

Education is often the first system in which families confront barriers. Schools provide more than academics. They offer therapy services, peer connections, structure, and a sense of purpose. Federal laws such as the Individuals with Disabilities Education Act (IDEA) and Section 504 of the Rehabilitation Act guarantee individualized support in the least restrictive environment. But legislation alone does not guarantee meaningful inclusion.

True advocacy in education requires understanding how a child's health, sensory processing, executive functioning, family dynamics, and trauma history shape their ability to learn. When Life Care Experts are involved, evaluations become more comprehensive, IEP and 504 goals align with medical realities, therapies are coordinated across settings, and transportation and safety plans reflect actual needs. The result is not just compliance but also a system that adapts to the child, rather than forcing the child to adapt to the system.

When schools fail to meet these obligations, families often feel powerless. Delays in evaluation, denials of accommodation, or claims that needs are "too complex" are common. At this stage, education attorneys may be essential. Seeking legal advocacy is not a sign of failure: it is a safeguard. By enforcing IDEA and Section 504, attorneys ensure that services reflect the child's needs, rather than the district's budget. Sometimes, school districts are even required to cover legal costs, making this an important tool when collaboration fails.

HEALTHCARE AND EDUCATION ARE NOT SEPARATE

Children with medical complexity often straddle both healthcare and educational systems, which rarely communicate effectively. A child with seizures, a feeding tube, or severe anxiety cannot participate in learning if their health needs are unmet. Life Care Experts bridge this divide by sharing relevant medical updates with schools, attending medical appointments, and aligning services across environments. Educational success begins with health stability.

THE TRANSITION TO ADULTHOOD

Perhaps the most difficult stage comes when school-based supports end. In childhood, the IEP provides structure, accountability, and a built-in team of professionals. When a student reaches age 18, or 21 in some states, that framework disappears. Families suddenly face a disjointed system of adult services while needing to make critical legal and financial decisions.

Transition planning involves multiple layers: identifying adult healthcare providers, exploring supported employment and housing, ensuring continuation of Medicaid or SSI, and deciding whether guardianship, power of attorney, or supported decision-making is appropriate. These choices determine whether the young adult's autonomy is honored while still safeguarding well-being.

Guardianship may be necessary when an individual cannot safely make decisions independently, while powers of attorney or supported decision-making agreements may preserve greater independence. Regardless of the legal tool chosen, early planning with attorneys, trustees, and Life Care Experts prevents crisis and creates a smoother handoff into adulthood.

CASE STUDIES

LIAM'S STORY

Liam, an 8-year-old with cerebral palsy, had mobility and sensory needs that could have easily sidelined him in a traditional classroom. Instead, through a coordinated team that included his family, a Life Care Expert, educators, healthcare providers, and legal and financial professionals, his IEP became more than a document. It functioned as a living roadmap, His therapies were coordinated, his transportation adapted, and communication across systems was seamless. With this support, Liam thrived. He gained confidence, built friendships, and developed a love of learning. His parents, once overwhelmed, became empowered advocates prepared for the future.

THE TRANSITION CLIFF

Emma, a 19-year-old with autism, had been supported throughout childhood by a strong IEP team. Once she aged out of school, however, her family found themselves without guidance. Medicaid waiver applications stalled, her SSI benefits were jeopardized by paperwork errors, and her parents were unprepared for decide between the options of guardianship or power of attorney.

With the involvement of a Life Care Expert, Emma's family created a structured plan: securing supported employment services, clarifying legal authority through limited guardianship, and establishing a Supplemental Needs Trust funded by her grandparents for long-term stability. The intervention prevented Emma from falling into crisis and gave her parents confidence that her adult life would be safe and purposeful.

A CULTURAL SHIFT IN PROFESSIONAL SUPPORT

Supporting children with special needs requires more than piecemeal solutions. It calls for an integrated approach in which medical, educational, financial, and legal systems align. Families should not be left to navigate these complexities alone. Trustees, attorneys, and wealth managers who partner with Life Care Experts provide continuity, ensuring that advocacy, planning, and care evolve seamlessly across the lifespan.

What if the measure of success was not how well a child fits into fragmented systems but how well those systems adapt to support the child? Supporting families of children with special needs means building structures that protect dignity, expand opportunity, and carry forward into adulthood. For professionals, the responsibility is not only financial stewardship but also the creation of frameworks that allow families to move from fear and exhaustion toward confidence and stability.

KEY CONSIDERATIONS FOR PROFESSIONALS

Supporting children with special needs is not only about meeting immediate challenges. It is about creating structures that last. Attorneys, trustees, and professionals play a critical role in protecting benefits, managing resources wisely, and ensuring that families are not left to navigate systems in isolation. Asking the right questions, coordinating with care professionals, and recognizing the individuality of each child establishes stability that endures beyond the capacity of parents or guardians.

For professionals, the message is clear: you are not simply managing finances or paperwork. You are shaping the framework that allows a child to thrive, a family to breathe, and a future to remain secure.

PART FIVE

BEST PRACTICES

The final part brings the lessons together, offering clear strategies that professionals can adopt as best practices. By applying a proactive, dignity-centered approach, professionals and advisors can shift from crisis containment to true partnership. This section translates ideas into actions that strengthen systems, protect trust integrity, and preserve quality of life.

CHAPTER 26

CRAFTING PATHWAYS TO DIGNITY: BEST PRACTICES FOR PROFESSIONALS

RETHINKING RESPONSIBILITY

What if compliance were understood not as the ceiling of fiduciary duty but as the floor—the necessary baseline rather than the measure of excellence? What if success was measured not only by whether decisions are defensible on paper but also by whether they protect the humanity of the person at the center?

These questions sit at the intersection of legal planning, financial management, and human care. Documents provide structure, but their impact depends on how well intention is translated into the lived quality of life. At their best, fiduciary systems are more than financial instruments. They are promises that resources will be used to safeguard dignity, create opportunity, and protect well-being over the long term.

No family who contacts my office is ever seeking to accumulate great wealth. What they want is safety and the quality of life that resources can provide. Yet sometimes, the compliance mindset in our industries creates the illusion that preserving wealth itself is the goal. How can professionals fulfill their duty without focusing on both quality of life and compliance?

THE LIMITS OF COMPLIANCE ALONE

Compliance is essential. Attorneys must uphold legal frameworks. Trustees must steward assets with diligence. Financial professionals must meet regulatory standards. These responsibilities form the backbone of our legal and financial systems.Yet compliance alone does not ensure quality of life. Even when every estate planning and financial checklist are complete, clients may still face isolation, exploitation, or preventable decline. By integrating a structured quality-of-life framework, professionals move from meeting minimum standards to safeguarding dignity.

Too often, estate plans are expertly drafted but remain static. Even when compliance is satisfied, opportunities for independence, skills, relationships, and community connections go unrecognized. Financial stewardship alone is not enough. Human insight, proactive oversight, and coordinated planning are what transform documents into lifelines.

EXPANDING THE TOOLKIT

Traditional planning instruments can be reframed as dynamic systems that protect both assets and dignity. Best practice includes the following:

- **Trusts and wills.** Treat them as more than asset transfers. Pair them with care memos or letters of intent that communicate values and wishes beyond money.
- **Powers of attorney.** Define expectations so agents understand that decisions must reflect quality of life, as well as risk management.
- **Healthcare proxies and HIPAA releases.** Add care values statements so proxies know what matters most, not only what is authorized.
- **Guardianships and conservatorships.** When necessary, include accountability mechanisms that safeguard rights and dignity.
- **Special Needs Trusts and ABLE accounts.** Review them regularly and collaborate with Life Care Experts so funds support goals, rather than remain unused.

- **Trust protectors.** Position them to guard quality-of-life intent, not only financial integrity.

Used with intention, these tools shift from static paperwork to active frameworks for stability.

THE VALUE OF LIFE CARE EXPERTS

Across the case studies and practices in this book, certain patterns are clear. Professionals bring legal authority and financial stewardship. Life Care Experts bring assessment, system navigation, and person-centered planning. Together, they bridge the gap between paper and lived experience.

Plans evolve when in-person assessments, benefit reviews, and clinical insights inform financial and legal decisions. Families may not know what support is available to them. Life Care Experts add depth by asking better questions, seeing risks before they escalate, and aligning care strategies with fiduciary intent.

CASE EXAMPLE: A PREVENTABLE CRISIS

Michael was 72 years old and living with advancing Parkinson's disease. His trust was well drafted, and his bills were paid on time. On paper, the trust satisfied fiduciary requirements. In reality, he was isolated, missing medications, and experiencing frequent falls that went unaddressed.

A Life Care Expert conducted a home visit and identified the gaps. The care plan was updated, a medication dispenser was installed, and regular aides were added for safety. Within months, his falls decreased, his health stabilized, and trust resources were applied in ways that preserved both safety and dignity.

These changes did not require more funds or extraordinary intervention. Yet they made the difference between technical compliance and proactive oversight that protected the beneficiary's quality of life.

ANCHORING BEST PRACTICE

Professionals who adopt best practices treat quality of life as a standard, not an afterthought. Their work is marked by:

- Centering the individual's goals and dignity in every decision.
- Using compliance as a baseline while also measuring quality of life.
- Establishing regular case reviews with written care plans, clear roles, and timelines.
- Monitoring proactively rather than waiting for crises.
- Collaborating across legal, financial, clinical, and family roles so silos do not compromise stability.
- Updating plans continuously as needs evolve.
- Leveraging technology to extend safety, independence, and oversight.

- Documenting decisions in ways that are both legally defensible and morally credible.

MEASURING SUCCESS

A system succeeds when the following occurs:

- The person's life is safe, stable, and fulfilling.
- Public benefits remain intact where relevant.
- Resources are used wisely and transparently.
- Autonomy and dignity are protected.
- Plans adapt in time, not only after a preventable crisis.

REFRAMING BEST PRACTICE

The old paradigm defined professional practice as asset protection plus compliance. The new paradigm calls for measuring quality of life with the same seriousness as compliance. Compliance sets the floor. Together, we can raise the standard to include dignity and quality of life, and we can make them measurable.

Through each chapter, we have seen where systems break down: families are left without guidance, professionals are caught in crises, and the dignity and stability of clients are overlooked. What has been missing is a way to bring those lessons together in one practical framework. The Solutions for Dignity® Life Care Framework™ was built for this purpose, turning best practice into measurable standards that align attorneys, trustees, and care experts around one shared responsibility: protecting dignity.

A CALL FORWARD

Do not stop at compliance.

Do not assume that assets alone protect well-being.

Do not wait for crisis to expose the gaps.

Protect assets.

Ensure compliance.

With equal seriousness, safeguard quality of life.

The Solutions for Dignity® Life Care Framework™ offers a way forward, using many of the systems outlined in this book. It will succeed when professionals lead, align documents with lived reality, raise standards, and protect not only files but lives. If you would like to learn more about The Solutions for Dignity® Life Care Framework™ please connect with our office as we pilot the measurable best practices outlined in this book in Pittsburgh, Pennsylvania.

Dignity should never be optional. It should be the standard. **Fiduciaries protect with prevention. Be the smoke detector, not the fire department.**

THE END

HOW TO USE THESE APPENDIXES

These appendixes provide a quick reference and practical toolkit. The glossary defines common terms you may encounter. The references point to sources for deeper exploration. The resources list national organizations that can provide guidance. The last appendix provides information about Life Care Expert pricing models. Always verify the information and consult qualified professionals for specific cases.

APPENDIX A

GLOSSARY OF TERMS

- **ABLE Account -** A tax-advantaged savings tool that allows individuals with disabilities to save for qualified expenses without affecting eligibility for means-tested benefits such as SSI and Medicaid.

- **Activities of Daily Living (ADLs) -** Basic self-care tasks including bathing, dressing, eating, toileting, transferring, and continence.

- **Adult Protective Services (APS) -** State and local agencies that investigate abuse, neglect, and exploitation of vulnerable adults and provide protective services.

- **Advance Directive -** Legal documents specifying medical care preferences and designated decision makers if individuals cannot make decisions for themselves.

- **Aging in Place -** Living safely and comfortably in one's home and community with needed supports.

- **Americans with Disabilities Act (ADA) -** Federal civil rights law prohibiting disability discrimination and requiring equal access to employment, public accommodations, government services, transportation, and telecommunications.

- **Assisted Living -**Residential care with personal care services, meals, and activities for individuals who need some assistance but not skilled nursing.

- **Care Coordination -** Organized collaboration among participants in a person's care to facilitate appropriate services.

- **Catastrophic Injury -** Severe injury causing permanent disability and long-term care needs.

- **Cognitive Impairment -** Decline in cognitive abilities that affects daily functioning.

- **Conservatorship -** Court appointment of a person or entity to manage financial affairs for someone unable to do so.

- **Dementia -** Broad term for cognitive decline that

interferes with daily life, including Alzheimer's disease and other forms.

- **Durable Power of Attorney -** Authority granted to another person to make financial or healthcare decisions, remaining effective during incapacity.

- **Elder Abuse -** Physical, emotional, sexual, or financial abuse, as well as neglect, abandonment, or self-neglect, of older adults.

- **Guardianship -** Court appointment of a guardian to make personal, medical, and/or financial decisions for someone lacking capacity.

- **Home and Community-Based Services (HCBS) -** Supports delivered in home and community settings rather than institutions.

- **Hospice Care -** Care focusing on comfort and quality of life for individuals with terminal illnesses.

- **Individualized Education Program (IEP) -** Written plan documenting a student's needs, goals, and services under IDEA.

- **Individuals with Disabilities Education Act (IDEA) -** Federal law ensuring free appropriate public education in the least restrictive environment.

- **Life Care Expert -** A professional who coordinates services across legal, financial, healthcare, and social domains for complex cases.

- **Long-Term Care -** Services and supports for individuals with limited ability to perform ADLs independently.

- **Long-Term Care Insurance -** Insurance that helps pay for services such as nursing homes, assisted living, and home care.

- **Medicaid -** Federal and state program providing healthcare coverage for eligible low-income individuals, including long-term care.

- **Medicare -** Federal health insurance primarily for people age 65 and older, and some younger people with disabilities.

- **Neurodivergent -** A term for individuals whose neurological functioning differs from typical patterns, including autism and ADHD.

- **Palliative Care -** Specialized medical care focused on relief from symptoms and stress of serious illness.

- **Person-Centered Planning -** Planning that centers on the individual's goals, preferences, and choices.

- **Representative Payee -** A person or organization appointed to manage Social Security or SSI benefits for a beneficiary.

- **Social Security Disability Insurance (SSDI) -** Monthly benefits for individuals who have paid Social Security taxes and can no longer work due to disability.

- **Special Needs Trust -** A trust that allows funds to be set aside for a person with disabilities without affecting eligibility for benefits.

- **Supplemental Security Income (SSI) -** Monthly payments to individuals with limited income and resources who are aged, blind, or disabled.

- **Supported Decision Making -** An alternative to guardianship that provides support for individuals to make their own decisions.

- **Undue Influence -** The use of trust or authority to override another person's free will.

APPENDIX B

REFERENCES

- **Administration for Community Living. How Much Care Will You Need? U.S. Department of Health and Human Services:** https://acl.gov/ltc/basic-needs/how-much-care-will-you-need

- **AARP. Middle-Income Boomers and Long-Term Care Planning:** https://www.aarp.org

- **American College of Trust and Estate Counsel (ACTEC): The Rising Trend of Trust and Estate Litigation:** https://actecfoundation.org

- **Centers for Medicare & Medicaid Services (CMS). Hospital Readmissions Reduction Program:** https://www.cms.gov/medicare/medicare-fee-for-service-payment/acuteinpatientpps/readmissions-reduction-program

- **Investopedia. Long-Term Care Planning: It Is About Family:** https://www.investopedia.com
- **National Council on Aging. Resources for Aging and Caregiving:** https://www.ncoa.org

APPENDIX C

RECOMMENDED RESOURCES

These resources are a starting point. Inclusion does not imply endorsement.

NATIONAL RESOURCES

- **Administration for Community Living (ACL):** https://acl.gov
- **National Council on Aging (NCOA):** https://www.ncoa.org
- **Social Security Administration (SSA):** https://www.ssa.gov
- **Centers for Medicare & Medicaid Services (CMS):** https://www.cms.gov

- **Substance Abuse and Mental Health Services A dministration (SAMHSA):** https://www.samhsa.gov Helpline: 1-800-662-HELP

- **National Alliance on Mental Illness (NAMI):** https://www.nami.org

- **The Arc:** https://thearc.org

- **ABLE National Resource Center:** https://www.ablenrc.org

LEGAL AND FINANCIAL PLANNING

- **ABA Commission on Law and Aging:** https://www.americanbar.org/groups/law_aging

- **ACTEC Foundation:** https://actecfoundation.org

- **National Academy of Elder Law Attorneys (NAELA):** https://www.naela.org

- **Special Needs Alliance:** https://www.specialneedsaliance.org

- **The National Elder Law Foundation (NELF):** https://www.nelf.org/attorney-directory-

CARE AND COMMUNITY SUPPORT

- **Family Caregiver Alliance (FCA):** https://www.caregiver.org
- **AARP Caregiving Resource Center:** https://www.aarp.org/caregiving
- **National Consumer Voice for Quality Long-Term Care:** https://theconsumervoice.org
- **Eldercare Locator:** https://eldercare.acl.gov

CRISIS AND EMERGENCY

- **988 Suicide and Crisis Lifeline:** Call or text 988 | https://988lifeline.org
- **SAMHSA Helpline:** 1-800-662-HELP (4357)

APPENDIX D

UNDERSTANDING LIFE CARE EXPERT PRICING MODELS

Pricing should be transparent. It should reflect the consistency, accountability, and depth required to prevent crises and sustain outcomes. The rates below apply to typical cases. Complex crisis work costs more. When multiple domains are in flux, first-year crisis services can range from $30,000–$90,000.

It's important to recognize that the rates in this book are not theoretical. They are drawn from my company's active caseload, from real invoices and negotiated contracts. For professionals making fiduciary decisions, this means the costs outlined here reflect what is truly happening in practice—the real dollars at stake when prevention is ignored and crises take hold.

BILLING MODELS

1. **Hourly Rates**

- Common range: **$135–$250 per hour**, depending on region, provider, and complexity.
- Covers assessments, coordination, family meetings, medical advocacy, and crisis work.

2. **Retainers or Packages**

- Initial retainers of **$2,500–$3,000**, drawn down as services are provided.
- Larger retainers may support Medicaid spend-down strategies.
- Service packages with defined annual or monthly hours include deliverables such as a written care plan and scheduled check-ins.

3. **Assessments and Intake**

- Flat fee of **$2,000–$3,500** for a home visit, history review, and customized written plan.

4. **Crisis and After-Hours Premiums**

- Crisis or urgent work is often billed at **double the standard rate**.

- Routine after-hours work is billed at **time-and-a-half**.

5. **Travel and Administrative Fees**

- Travel billed at full or half rate; mileage reimbursed at the IRS rate.

- Documentation and coordination time billed.

6. **Membership or Subscription Models**

- Monthly fees covering limited proactive oversight, with additional hours billed as needed.

A SPECIAL THANK YOU

A heartfelt thank you to the professionals and colleagues who reviewed early drafts of this book. Your feedback, real-world perspective, and encouragement strengthened the work and refined its message.

- Jeff Ash, Rivers Community Fiduciary Services
- Colleen Bratkovich, Zacharia, Brown & Bratkovich
- Susan Cardello, Julian Gray & Associates
- Brian Carroll, Bank of New York Mellon
- Jackie Connell, Merrill Lynch
- Sunny Erdman, Shorebridge Wealth Management
- Rich Howard, Rivers Community Fiduciary Services

• Matthew Kikta, Julian Gray & Associates

• Colin May, The Estate Planning Centers at Coulter & May, PC

• Eric O'Connor, Rivers Community Fiduciary Services

• Elizabeth Poggi, Smithfi eld Trust

• Karen Stollar, PNC Private Bank

• Matthew Thiel, Signature Wealth

• Eric Vogt, Waldron Private Wealth

Your partnership, collaboration, and shared commitment to this work makes progress possible.

ABOUT THE AUTHOR

For the last fifteen years, Patricia A. Hanson, LPC, co-owner and managing director of a life management organization in Pittsburgh, Pennsylvania, has worked supporting older adults, individuals with disabilities, and children with special needs alongside a team of highly skilled Life Care Experts. Her work focuses on medical advocacy, care management, and addressing routine living concerns as they intersect with law and finance.

Through this work, Patricia has seen how unmet needs often go unrecognized until they become crisis. Over the last six years, she has dedicated her efforts to developing the Solutions for Dignity® Life Care Framework™, a structured model designed to bridge the gap between what is written in professional plans and what people actually need to live with dignity.

The Framework introduces measurable best practices that align clinical insight, professional responsibility, and real-world needs, creating a clear path for professionals and families to address quality of life, reduce risks, and preserve dignity.

Patricia lives in Pennsylvania with her family and continues to lead conversations that challenge professionals to redefine what it means to protect wealth, dignity, and quality of life.

BRIDGING
THE GAP

www.ingramcontent.com/pod-product-compliance
Lightning Source LLC
LaVergne TN
LVHW060030210926
848481LV00013B/3832
* 9 7 9 8 9 0 2 2 3 6 3 1 3 *